MW01115509

Adapt
Or
Perish

Featuring:

Ilene Albert-Nelson
Steve Amos
Mark Fierle
John Hall
Lee Pound
Murray Schrantz
VaNessa Vollmer
Emily Woodman-Nance

www.adaptorperishbook.com
www.adaptorperishblog.com

Adapt or Perish!

Published by Solutions Press
4533 MacArthur Blvd., #200
Newport Beach, CA 92660

First edition printed June 2011

ISBN: 978-0-9827646-4-0

Printed in the United States of America

This is a work of non-fiction. The ideas presented are those of each author alone. All references to possible income to be gained from the techniques discussed in this book relate to specific past examples and are not necessarily representative of any future results specific individuals may achieve.

Table of Contents

Preface		Lee Pound	v

Part I: Adapting Business   **1**

1	The Power of Why	Ilene Albert-Nelson	3
2	Company of "Me"	Emily Woodman-Nance	7
3	The Entrepreneurial Job	Lee Pound	17
4	Why Social Media is Changing Everything	Ilene Albert-Nelson	23
5	Taking the Mystery Out of Social Media	Lee Pound	29
6	Strengths of a Company or Person	Mark Fierle	35
7	Resiliency Keys to Success for Individuals and Organizations	VaNessa Vollmer, Psy.D.	39
8	Being Outrageous to Succeed	Steve Amos	59
9	Generation Trends in the Workforce	VaNessa Vollmer, Psy.D.	63
10	Human Resources Professionals as Coaches	Emily Woodman-Nance	77
11	Training by Tribal Knowledge	VaNessa Vollmer, Psy.D.	81
12	Military Succession Planning Lessons for the Business Community	Murray Schrantz	91

| **13** | Hiring an Executive Recruiter | Mark Fierle | 101 |

Part II: Adapting Leadership   111

14	Becoming the Risk Averse Organization	Ilene Albert-Nelson	113
15	Being a Risk Taker	Steve Amos	117
16	Personal and Professional Development Applied	VaNessa Vollmer, Psy.D.	121
17	The Succession Minded Employee	Murray Schrantz	137
18	How to Work in a Virtual Organization	Ilene Albert-Nelson	145
19	The Challenge of Managing Virtual Organizations	Ilene Albert-Nelson	149
20	Music, Nature and Successful Organization Commonality	VaNessa Vollmer, Psy.D.	155
21	Finding Unique Solutions	Steve Amos	163
22	Creating Teams in Corporate Communities	VaNessa Vollmer, Psy.D.	167

Part III: Adapting Careers   173

23	Knowledge of the Effects of Job Loss	Emily Woodman-Nance	175
24	Dealing with Job Loss and the Social Support System	VaNessa Vollmer, Psy.D.	181
25	Preparing for Job Change	Mark Fierle	191

26	Financial Adaptation: What's Your Burn Rate?	VaNessa Vollmer, Psy.D.	195
27	Making a Great First Impression	Steve Amos	207
28	Adapt or Stagnate	John Hall	213
29	What happens when the recruiter calls?	Mark Fierle	223
	Afterword	VaNessa Vollmer, Psy.D.	235
	Meet the Authors		239

"*Adapt or Perish* is an impressive breadth of topics covered by knowledgeable industry experts sharing their insights, aha moments and research. This is a must read for those facing transition and more important for those managing people that have been through transition. I appreciated the chapter on "Generation Trends" and was able to relate it to personal, social and work situations giving me a new perspective of how to better influence, motivate and build teams; for example, the benefits of pairing generations within a team. The reference list of supporting material is likewise impressive and adds credence to the material presented in the book. It is unlikely I'll read all of the references and, after reading this book, likely won't have to. Thank you for this wonderful compilation in *Adapt or Perish*."

Donald Baddorf
Vice President, Investment Solutions

"Find out what it takes to succeed in the new normal. From managing social media to managing your career, from understanding generational tendencies to managing risk, this book is a road map to a successful future for individuals and organizations. Filled with valuable charts and easy exercises, it will help you take control and move forward."

Eugenie R. Brown
VP Business Development

"You capture the essence of what it means to survive dealing with job loss and achieve ongoing success in life. I especially enjoyed the sections referring to professional responsibility, motivating people and resiliency. Furthermore, the personal references spoke to me such as 'make happy moments' and 'I'm going to be OK.' Thank you team!"

Marilyn L. Burtt, MBA

"Change is one characteristic that separates the good talent from the great talent. As an executive recruiter, the companies I work with want people that can adapt to change and do it quickly. The blend of the authors' experiences and coaching is valuable for all levels of an organization, including CEOs. I will encourage the people I work with to read this book. The title says it all."

Brad Remillard
IMPACT Hiring Solutions

"So many 'self-help' books preach, ramble, and simply leave us with a sense of having wasted our time. *Adapt or Perish* is a rare combination of identifying the key areas of need yet keeping it light and interesting. It is a book you can easily read in an afternoon that might change your life forever. It features subject matter experts who succinctly shared their expertise **and** provided tangible exercises, which showed me what well-developed thought was given to this book."

Cindy Pickens, Founder, CaféNet
regional networking organization

"*Adapt or Perish* is a great collection of valuable information from very credible sources. Bringing together the wisdom of so many renowned experts provides information in a single resource that generally requires sifting through dozens of books."

Nancy Salzman, Esq.,
Dean, Extended Education
Brandman University

"I think *Adapt or Perish* will be a very valuable read for managers at all levels including small business."

Lt. Col. Gene Wolf
(Former Commander) Squadron 40
California Wing - Civil Air Patrol
Auxiliary U.S. Air Force

"Change is a constant theme in business and this book gives us answers! What a refreshing set of topics and talented authors. A must read for any entrepreneur or executive."

Mark J. Kohler, CPA, Attorney,
Author of **What Your CPA Isn't Telling You**

"This step by step guidebook takes you through the process of embracing changes in business. It provides you with useful tools and tips for personal development by finding the ideal position."

Gwen Bernal, Human Resources Executive

"*Adapt or Perish* could also have been titled *Thrive or Perish*. Each chapter in this book has great information and ideas about how to make the changes necessary to succeed in the current business environment. There is red meat here for business owners, C-level executives, directors, and managers as well as those seeking their next position. I highly recommend *Adapt or Perish* for all who want to succeed in our changing business environment."

Richard Horstmeyer, MD,
Past President of Experience Unlimited

Preface

By Lee Pound

The phrase "Adapt or Perish" has more meaning today than it ever has in the past. Has business ever changed faster than today? Whole markets appear overnight, and established companies disappear by acquisition, consolidation or bankruptcy. How do these changes affect you?

Change is part of life. Sometimes it's pleasurable, others feared, and most of the time it creates opportunities.

Every generation since the dawn of time has faced changes in the way they live, the way they do business, find food, and relate to their fellow human beings. For some generations, this change has been very small, for others it has been huge.

Today we live in an era of constant change. For instance, my grandmother was born in 1878 and grew up riding in horse-drawn buggies. On her 91st birthday, she watched the first men land on the moon.

Since then, change has accelerated. New technologies arrive, flash into brilliance and then fade into obscurity in years, not decades or centuries. Like most change, many people and businesses ignore it, try to avoid it and then eventually accept parts of it. Many others never accept it and become irrelevant.

Those who succeed adapt their businesses to use these changes to their advantage. Others, and the examples are numerous, refuse to accept change, do what they've always done, and eventually disappear. For instance, buggy makers in 1900 said people would never accept the automobile. They vanished. Businesses such as

Blockbuster built industries around video tape rentals and sales and with new technologies arriving almost daily, find themselves near bankruptcy.

The lesson is that we've always had change. Past generations dealt with one, maybe two major changes in their lifetimes. In the 20th Century the pace picked up. The last generation saw dozens of major changes in the way society worked, the way information was distributed, and in the way we as individuals related to each other.

Our generation faces hundreds of changes in very short periods of time. We live today as no other generation has lived. We have access to more information, more diverse people and potential customers, and more parts of the world than ever before.

Here are a few of the new technologies that have become available in the last few years:

- **Digital libraries.** Google and others have digitized books, articles, and manuscripts that were only available in physical archives and made them available to everyone.
- **Music business.** Cheap digital downloads have changed the way music publishers do business and the way musicians make money.
- **Publishing.** New digital printing technologies have made book publishing accessible to everyone for just a few hundred dollars.
- **Networking.** Digital social networks such as Twitter, Facebook and LinkedIn allow people to make instant connections all over the world and meet people they could never have met as late as five years ago.
- **Marketing.** Finding and targeting customers has never been easier for businesses and professionals.
- **Blogs and Videos.** Getting your message out has never been easier. Everyone with an opinion can express it publicly and get an audience, large or small. Everyone can be on video thanks to inexpensive cameras and free delivery methods.
- **Job Searches and Employee Recruiting.** The Internet has made so much information available so quickly that a Google search is one of the first steps both job seekers and employers take. Those who don't show up are increasingly irrelevant.

With this increased speed of change has come a decrease in planning for the future. We are so uncertain about what will happen five years from now that both individuals and corporations seldom plan more than a few months in advance. Corporations are obsessed with the next quarter's results. Politicians don't think past the next election. Employees have no idea what their next job will be.

In *Adapt or Perish*, we make the point that change is an opportunity. Those who embrace the latest technologies will make fortunes. Those who plan beyond the moment, who make room for adding new technologies as they appear, who have a long-term vision for their future, will be the leaders of tomorrow. Job seekers who stand out from the crowd of competitors will get the best positions. Those who build strong relationships will be the new influencers.

In the midst of accelerating change, we sometimes forget that new technologies are not new things that we must do. They are simply new ways of doing what we have always done. People have always created relationships, started businesses, marketed themselves, gotten jobs, expressed opinions, done research, read books, and traveled. We will continue to do all of these. The difference is that if we do them in the old-fashioned way, we will stay stuck in the middle of a crowd of competitors. We will fall behind. We will become as irrelevant as the horse and buggy.

When we are in the forefront of change, we become the new leaders. We stand out in ways we never dreamed possible.

Adapt or Perish will change your life. It will make you aware of new ideas, new possibilities, new ways of thinking, and new ways to become the new leaders of tomorrow. Read with care, implement with courage, and you will reap the rewards.

"This book addresses the ongoing challenges of adapting to change without fear of failure in an ever increasing social media presence within an electronic age of information. The in-depth insight of adapting the vision of the business model, continuous strategic planning coupled with the importance of the selection leaders are addressed in a compelling manner for a world ever so transitioning to a transactional based global economic model. A must read."

COL(R) Edward G. Carson, Chief Executive Officer,
Growth Management and Constructive Changes, LLC

"This book will give new and seasoned business professionals insightful strategies for adapting and thriving in a constantly changing global marketplace."

Beverly Jones, Higher Education Administrator

"*Adapt or Perish* is a book for everyone who would like to succeed in this fast changing world. Look for the opportunities that exist in the change, embrace it and become the leader of tomorrow."

Sushma Rajput
Toastmasters Founder's District
Public Relations Chair, Div F 2010-2011

"*Adapt or Perish* is a comprehensive collection of wisdom and advice from some of the nation's leading experts on change. Their perspectives on successfully leading organizations through an environment of shifting landscapes equip the reader to effectively adapt in business, leadership, and in careers. Where continuous change is now the new normal, *Adapt or Perish* is a guidebook on change management that deserves to be in every executive's library."

Frank Borst, President & CEO at Masterpiece Consulting

Section 1

Adapting Business

Making Your Company Stronger

1

The Power of Why

By Ilene Albert-Nelson

"Why?" is the most powerful question you can ask yourself both about what you do and what your company does. It doesn't matter whether it involves a process, a strategy, or the way you or your company reacts to challenge and adversity.

"Why?" can also be a tough question if you don't want to face the answers, especially if you are facing life changing issues such as a job search or dramatic changes in your industry.

When your personal life or your company or industry changes or established processes don't work, "Why?" may be the most important question you can ask. Even when your life or business is going well, asking why may help you make it better.

For You

When was the last time you took a critical look at your life goals and asked yourself, "Why am I doing this?" or "Why is this important" or "Why do I care about this?" When was the last time you challenged your thinking about career goals?

Many of us choose our careers because we got our first job in that field or because our parents worked in that career. However, is that what you are best suited to do or passionate about? Is your behavior getting you what you want or is it sabotaging your efforts? Is what you are doing giving you satisfaction or joy? Why are you doing it if it isn't satisfying? Remember, there is an old saying, "If you keep doing what you have been doing, you will keep getting what you have gotten."

People don't ask why because they are scared to challenge the status quo. If you have been successful in your career, it is even scarier to admit that what you are doing isn't what you want to do.

What happens when change happens around you? The current economy won't allow many people to keep doing what they have done in the past. Companies have permanently eliminated many jobs and many industries will lag behind in job creation for years to come. Still, many people are looking for work in these industries or expecting to find the same job they had before using the same search methods they used 5 or 10 years ago.

Change is hard. It's also the most important thing you can do if you want more success and happiness. If your current efforts aren't working, ask "Why?" and change them!

For Your Company

Anyone can ask "Why?" about what your company does but it can be difficult to get your organization to change. Challenging it in a positive way can lead to rewards as long as you are willing to assume responsibility for making change happen. Pointing fingers and complaining won't solve the problem. Asking why and proposing solutions will.

When was the last time you challenged your company to change? "Why?" is a very powerful way to focus activity and strategy. Just because the company has always done it that way in the past doesn't mean that it should continue to do so in the future.

Always ask at least five levels of "Why?" to find the underlying root cause of a problem (Method developed by Sakichi Toyoda at Toyota Motor Corporation -Wikipedia). This helps you understand the nature of the problem and the solution. In some cases, you may find even deeper layers and may face multiple issues. Asking why and gathering diverse opinions allows the organization to come to grips with key issues and not just resolve symptoms.

Be the person who asks good questions and proposes solutions and you will become a thought leader in your company and will drive growth and profitability. In today's climate, both are critical components for business success.

If you don't challenge the status quo, you may find your company or your position outmoded, out of date and potentially out of business.

Don't fear the question!

6 Adapt or Perish

2

Company of "ME"

By Emily Woodman-Nance

Ever wonder what separates the good from the great?

The biggest difference is the mindset of the great. Successful people take personal responsibility for their lives. Where does it start? With first acknowledging that you will always be in charge of one aspect of your life – YOURSELF! If you relinquish this responsibility, someone else will set the course for your life, which means that your life will not have true purpose and meaning.

This new paradigm of personal responsibility is more crucial than ever for the current workforce. Gone are the days of job security, a pension, and lifelong benefits. People have fewer opportunities and a deep sense of despair.

James Agee said, "You must be in tune with the times and be prepared to break with tradition." It's time to shift your mindset if you want to successfully maneuver in today's new job market. Think of yourself as a company. The product you are marketing is your skill set. For your business to compete at an optimal level in a saturated market, several essential elements need to be in place:

- Powerful vision
- Mission statement
- Continuous strategic planning

- Shrewd Board of Directors
- Value added product
- Checks and balances
- System for taking care of the owner of the company – YOU
- Exit strategy

Create a Powerful Vision

Have you ever been around people who wander aimlessly through life? There's a good reason. They have no vision.

Numerous experts on leadership and personal development emphasize how vital it is to construct a personal vision for your life. Warren Bennis, Stephen Covey, Peter Senge, and others point out that a powerful vision can help you succeed far beyond what you could do without one.

Your vision statement guides your life. It provides the direction necessary to make choices about your career. Your vision statement is a light shining in the darkness which guides you on your way. In its simplest essence a vision statement is a long-term view of the future. It answers the question, "What aspirations do I have for the world in which I operate and what do I have some influence over?"

Creating your vision statement will require introspection and uninterrupted time. Using this exercise will give your a jump-start to creating your vision.

Find an isolated area. Picture yourself two years from now.

- What are you doing?
- What have you accomplished?
- What is important to you?

Now imagine that you are being profiled on the news. What are you recognized for?

Do not filter your responses. Write down what comes to mind and include as many details regarding your professional and personal life as you come up with. Remember, career is just one facet of your life. Don't neglect the personal.

Continue to refine your vision statement until it accurately reflects your vision of who you are.

To give your vision statement the most power, describe it in the present tense. Act as if it were already true.

Create Your Mission Statement

When I hear the words *mission statement*, the first thing that comes to mind is *Purpose*. You may have already had conversations about your purpose in life. Many best sellers, such as *The Purpose Driven Life* and *First Things First*, focus on purpose.

Even with all of this discussion and literature about purpose, for some discovering their purpose in life seems like an unsolvable mystery or a daunting prospect. Stephen Covey (in *First Things First*) refers to developing a mission statement as "connecting with your unique purpose and the profound satisfaction that comes from fulfilling it." Just think, discovering your mission is equivalent to a front seat view into who you are and what is important to you. Ultimately, it is an opportunity for the "real you to stand up."

Here are two reasons why finding your purpose in life is important:

- **It gives meaning to everything you do.** You could be a success but if you do not have meaning you will feel empty inside.
- **It motivates you.**

You may experience failure or rejection. In such situations, your life purpose can give you the motivation you need to keep going.

A mission statement allows you to identify companies that have similar values and beliefs and helps you to better assess the costs and benefits of any career opportunity.

Your mission statement supports your vision. Your vision is a view of the future, how you get there is your mission.

Here are five questions to help you compose your mission statement:

- What talents and gifts do I possess?
- What do I stand for? (Core values, i.e. tranquility, hope, etc.)
- What was I put on the earth to do?
- Who will I help?
- How will I make a difference?

Draft your mission statement using these words: "My mission is to." Continue to draft your mission statement until it provides the answer to your purpose for existing.

Once you have a mission that supports your vision, you can form goals that state how you will accomplish your mission.

10 Adapt or Perish

Setting goals can impact your earning power and your aspirations. So get ready to set goals.

Think about what you want your career to look like in one to two years, after the next five years, and at the end of your life.

What I want my career to look like in **1-2 YEARS**	What I want my career to look like in **5 YEARS**	What I want my career to look like by the end of my **LIFE**

Where are you today relative to your one to two year goals, the next five years, and your lifetime objectives?

What are your educational goals?

What specific experience do you need to reach your objectives?

To help you accomplish your goals, identify action steps and deadlines. The following template can be used to formulate your goals.

Goal Period: (i.e. short term – 1-2 years)

GOALS	ACTION STEPS	DEADLINES

Evaluate each goal and ensure it passes the **SMART** test:

S = Specific

M=Measurable

A=Attainable

R – Realistic

T = Timely (timeframe is set)

You now have a direction, a meaning and steps to achieve your aspirations. When a curve ball comes your way, you can address it in a way that aligns with your vision and mission.

Engage in Continuous Strategic Planning

In the literature about why businesses fail, one of the top reasons is lack of planning. Many business owners and people are so eager to get started that they neglect to plan and jump in head first. Your plan is your blueprint for success. A well thought out plan forces you to think about the future and the challenges you will face. It forces you to consider your financial needs, your marketing and management plans, your competition, and your overall strategy for coming out on top. According to the Small Business Administration, a plan should consist of the following four sections:

1. Description of the business
2. Marketing
3. Finances
4. Management

As a business, the description will consist of your vision and mission statements. Marketing includes the collateral materials, personal branding, and marketing media you will use to get the word out about who you are and what you can do. Focusing on finances will allow you to determine how much cash reserve is necessary based on market trends. A budget is crucial for your business to expand and operate smoothly. Management is about staying active with seminars, training, and checking the job market periodically. Your plan is a living document that requires continuous updating and review.

It is important to always know where you stand financially. The budget template below will assist in developing a financial snapshot. Add appropriate income streams and expenses.

	Monthly	Comments
Income:		
Your Primary Income		
Your Spouse's Income		
Child Support or Alimony		

Other Income		
Total Monthly Income		
Necessary Expenses:		
Rent or Mortgage		
2nd Mortgage or Home Equity Loan		
Property Taxes		
Water		
Trash		
Gas and Electric		
Auto Insurance		
Healthcare or Insurance Costs		
Total Necessary Expenses		
Discretionary Expenses:		
Credit Card Bills		
Auto Loan (s)		
Gasoline		
Cable or Satellite TV		
Mobile Phone (s)		
Total Discretionary Expenses		
Investment Spending:		
401K, 403B deposits		
IRA deposits		
Employee Stock Plans		
Total Investment Spending		
TOTAL MONTHLY OUTGOING DIFFERENCE:(Income-Outgoing)		

If you discover a deficit, look at reserves and whether they can be used to offset the deficit. Your reserves are financial assets that you can quickly liquidate such as bank accounts, 401Ks and lines of credit.

Gather a Shrewd Board of Directors

For a business to successfully compete in a saturated market, it needs a keen board of directors. Likewise, to compete in today's job market you need a board of directors which will give you direction and support. Your board of directors can include the following:

- **Mentor.** Someone who has "been there done that."
- **Career Coach.** Can help you create your board of directors and serve on it.
- **Accountability partner.** To help you stay on track and give you support.
- **Realtor.** To advise you on your residential and/or commercial property.
- **Financial Advisor.** To advise you on the best financial choices.
- **Spiritual Advisor.** Can provide spiritual guidance and support.

You decide the composition of your board of directors. The key is to get members who are caring and competent as well as aligned with your values and your goals. Your board members are probably already in your network.

Value Added Product

The purpose of a company's product is to provide value and satisfy a desire of the buyer. According to the law of supply and demand, if there is an abundance of supply and the demand is low inventory is shelved or perishes. The same holds true with the job market. If there a more candidates than jobs, some people stay unemployed and others may completely check out of the workforce. Keep in mind that your product is your skill set. It is more important than ever that your skill set adds value to an organization and sets you apart from the competition. To keep competitive you can do the following:

- Stay abreast of industry/career trends
- Become involved in the professional organization(s) that are aligned with your career/industry
- Conduct informational interviews with successful people in your career/industry to find out what they are doing

- Constantly look at how you can add value to the company. Is there a problem you can solve?
- Train, train, train

Checks and Balances:

Review your plan on a regular basis to ensure that it is viable and that you are adding value to an organization. Experts recommend every 8-10 months, as long as everything is fairly stable. Since your plan contains specific dates and budgets you need to determine how often to review your plan. As a rule of thumb, the plan should always be updated when there are any major changes taking place. The obvious changes are job outlook, market trends and financial forecast.

Taking Care of the Owner of the Company – YOU:

When dealing with stress of any kind, the first thing that slips to the bottom of the list is YOU. You begin to operate at sub par levels. Taking care of yourself is essential to doing your very best in any situation. Here are some ways to take care of yourself:

- **Eat right.** Make sure you eat enough healthy foods.
- **Sleep.** Try to get 7-8 hours of sleep per night.
- **Exercise**. Research suggests people feel better after exercising.
- **Take time out for yourself**. Doing something enjoyable relieves stress and keeps your spirits up.
- **Keep your sense of humor.** This includes laughing at yourself.
- **Learn how to say no.** Know your limits and do not take on more than you can handle.
- **Avoid people who stress you out.** You know who they are. If you cannot turn the relationship around, limit your time with them.
- **Avoid hot-button topics.** If you get upset over a certain topic, stop bringing it up or excuse yourself when it comes up.

If you regularly make time for rest and relaxation, you will be in a better place to handle life's curve balls.

Exit Strategy:

Businesses incorporate exit strategies into their planning. An exit strategy, a plan to get out of a situation, is crucial in bringing about a positive conclusion to a business undertaking. As a business, your mission is to be in tune with the organization's culture and see in advance that it is time to prepare for an exit. To be in an optimal position for leaving an organization, do the following:

- Keep your resume current. Capture your successes as they unfold.
- Interview at least once a quarter. That way your interview skills are heightened and you stay aware of what other organizations want.
- Continue to network and remain visible for the day when you need to start a new job search.

Now you have tools to take personal responsibility for yourself and set the course for your career. Now more than ever, this is a great time to do something completely different or to consider entrepreneurship.

Joel Barker frames it quite nicely. "Vision without action is merely a dream. Action without vision just passes the time. Vision with action can change the world." Unlimited possibilities await you!

16 Adapt or Perish

3

The Entrepreneurial Job

By Lee Pound

It used to be that people entering the job market followed one of two very different career paths. They either got a job or started a business.

Those who got a job could look forward to a career that often included working for just one company, getting regular promotions, retirement at age 65 with a pension, and a good benefits package. They would make a decent salary or hourly wage, take home enough to buy that house that was always part of the American dream, and live in suburban communities surrounding major cities.

Those who started a business quickly learned how to market themselves and their businesses or didn't survive long. They often worked long hours for little pay, worried about cash flow, many times had no pension plan, took little money home, and faced economic ups and downs that could put them out of business.

They also created the jobs that the first group competed for, took the risks that in many cases led to great rewards, and provided the engine that powered the economy.

Those who had a job understood little about marketing unless that was their job. They occasionally changed jobs and when that happened went through a prescribed ritual that included writing resumes, sending them to potential employers, and waiting for responses.

The business owner, on the other hand, marketed all the time. However, when the time came to hire a new employee, he or she accepted resumes, checked out a few of them, tossed most of them, and hired the person who seemed to be the best fit.

The New Paradigm

Times have changed.

Over the last few decades, that lifetime job became more and more insecure. Employees were more likely to be hit by layoffs or downsizing. Companies treated their workers more as commodities than as integral parts of the operation. The number of jobs an employee holds in a lifetime increased until today the average length of a job is two and one-half to five years.

In this new job market, getting a job takes almost as long as the job itself will last. Finding the job has become more of a marketing campaign than a traditional job search. With many candidates for each position, people need to find new ways to stand out.

Marketing for the Job Seeker

Many people today move back and forth from traditional jobs to running their own businesses. Many out of work corporate executives become consultants, many to their old companies. Instead of sitting in their living rooms collecting unemployment and waiting for a job offer, they make new positions, whether salaried or contract, happen.

In the process, employees become more like the entrepreneurs they used to court for jobs and less like the old line employees who occasionally had to look for a new job.

These entrepreneurial skills are an important part of the new job seeking paradigm.

The Job Search Strategy

A job search strategy is much like a sales presentation. You must follow certain steps to differentiate yourself from the crowd, to catch the eye of a potential employer, and convince that employer that you are the one to do the job.

There are four steps to this new strategy:
1. Get their attention.

a. If nobody notices you, nobody will hire you. If all the resumes are the same, you will not stand out.

b. Create your message to the world and to potential employers. That message tells them what you can offer them. It is the benefit of hiring you.

c. Place that message where potential employers will find it. This will include social media sites.

d. Be findable on Google. Most employers will check potential employees on the Internet before calling for an interview. If your accomplishments are posted on sites such as YouTube, LinkedIn, Twitter and Facebook, they will appear in Google indexes and your potential employer will find them.

e. Research potential employers. Find out what their problems are, what their goals for the future are, what kind of employees they are looking for, and then make sure they know you can give them what they want.

f. Find potential employers on social media sites and connect with them. Ask them what they need and show them how you can help them meet that need.

2. Build your persona or character.

a. You have individual experiences, desires and talents that nobody else has. Unfortunately the traditional hiring process does not allow you to bring out these characteristics in a powerful way.

b. As an individual, you are unique. You are sum of everything you have done, all the companies you have worked for, and all of your personal accomplishments. You want something specific. Be very clear on what that is. Also be very clear that you will do what is necessary to get what you want.

3. What problems have you faced and overcome?

a. Tell your personal story in terms of what you wanted, the problems you faced in getting it and the steps you took to get it. These can be personal or work related as long as they relate to the problem you need to solve.

b. Show the strength of your perseverance. How much were you willing to risk for what you wanted? How did the problem you overcame relate to the problem your potential employer needs to overcome.

   c. Show the positive result of the actions that you took.

4. Ask for the job.

   a. This is the most important part of all. Show what you can do for the company then ask them to hire you to do it for them.

The Entrepreneurial Mindset

Even if you prefer to work for a company and continue to get salaried or hourly jobs rather than work for yourself, you must adopt certain mindsets. These mindsets offer a different way to think about how you get a job and how you get customers and clients.

1. **Your primary job is sales.** Before you can perform services for your clients you must first attract clients. Therefore much of your day is spent on marketing yourself to potential employers.

2. **Your primary client is your employer.** Once you have this client, your job is to keep the company satisfied with your contributions. A client will leave if you do not meet expectations. An employer will fire you if you do not perform.

3. **You must always be aware of where the next client is coming from.** Keep your eye on the future. Remember that your job will only last one or two years. Do you know where you want to go and what you want to do after this job is over? What skills will your next employer need and how can you get those skills while you are working here.

4. **Market yourself every day.** Make sure your Internet postings are up to date. Keep showing your expertise on social media sites. Keep your profiles up to date. Always have your current employer listed and always update your accomplishments.

5. **Build a list of hot prospects.** Keep adding potential employers to your database. Email them a newsletter with your latest thoughts and accomplishments. Keep them posted on trends in your field. Make sure they know who you are and what you do before you ever ask them to hire you.

6. **Update your skills and knowledge.** Keep attending seminars and workshops. Add skills you think you may need in the

future. Add skills your current employer needs, particularly in jobs one level above yours.

7. **Network with others in your profession.** There is no better way to get a job than to have someone who works there recommend you. Build contacts that know and like you long before you need to use them. Find out about potential job opportunities from these acquaintances.

8. **Do the best possible job you can for your current client (employer).** Always build bridges. Make your current boss your raving fan. Even if he lays you off in the future, you may get a great recommendation from him. Get testimonials from present and past bosses and place them on LinkedIn so future employers can find them.

9. **Leave your current job on good terms.** Even if you are fired, thank your boss for the job while you had it. Be gracious as you leave. Ask if you can use him or her as a reference. Make certain a glow of good feeling is always attached to your name.

10. **Never speak ill of a previous boss in a public place.** Facebook is no place to air your grievances. If you complain about how your previous company treated you, future possible employers will find it and take it into consideration when they interview you. Keep your public record spotless and positive.

11. **Always strive to serve people, even if you may never work for them.** The more you help others, the more your reputation will grow. People will talk glowingly of how you helped them and future employers will find those remarks and, again, take them into consideration during the hiring process.

Conclusion

Your most important client is you. Your job is to get that important client work that pays. When you treat yourself and your potential employers like valuable clients, you will create lifelong relationships that will help you in every step of your career.

22 Adapt or Perish

4

Why Social Media is Changing Everything for Businesses

By Ilene Albert-Nelson

There has been a lot of "ink" (both real and digital) spent on Social Media and why it is important. But many people still don't understand it and are afraid of it. Many businesses still aren't online even though their customers are. Here is why your business needs to be there too, especially if your company sells to consumers, is local in nature, or has a large pool of prospective customers. If you are a business-to-business company or have a very small customer pool, then Social Media may not be as critical for you. However, don't rule it out until you have checked it out!

Some Basic Facts

Facebook now has over 500 million users. This means that Facebook is larger than the US (which has about 305 million people). In fact, it is larger than all but two countries in the world! Fifty percent of active users sign in on any given day and 60 million update their status every day. People upload 3 BILLION photos each month and more than 5 BILLION pieces of content are uploaded every week. From a business perspective, more than 20 MILLION people become fans of a page every day. Average users spend 55 minutes a day on the site and become fans of four pages each month. In fact, some days Facebook outdraws Google! (Source: Facebook Press Room). And you aren't here interacting with this engaged, interested and willing audience?

Then there is Twitter, which has over 15 million users. Not all are active but many are and many more follow than tweet. And 23.5 million people visited the site worldwide. (People can check Twitter feeds without being a member.) 50 Million tweets are sent out every day. Twitter is the number 12 website in the world. (Source: The Next Web)

And then there is You Tube. You Tube is the fourth largest site on the web. They get 300 Million visitors worldwide per month. There are 5 Billion video streams every month. 15 hours of video are uploaded every MINUTE. And they have 3.5 million visitors per day. They are now the second largest search site on the web – bigger than Yahoo. (Source: Clean Cut Media) You Tube allows you to share videos about your business with the world. Embedded links in your website or blog can be shared with You Tube.

So why should your business be on these sites or others? The biggest reason is that these sites are the top sites on the web today after Google. Facebook has had days when it exceeded Google as the most used site on the web! (Google, Facebook, Yahoo, MSN, You Tube are the top 5 sites in March 2010 – Source: Quantcast.com).

These sites are where your customers spend their time today, not where they have been in the past. Traditional media is still useful but is declining and declining rapidly for younger consumers.

Here are some of the reasons, advantages and key learning items for Social Media for business.

- Your customers and consumers are on social media and aren't consuming traditional media the way they used to. Here are some statistics about traditional media:
  o Newspapers are declining rapidly – consumers are increasingly turning to the internet and 24-hour cable news. Have you looked at the size of your daily

newspaper lately? Ad revenue has dropped 27% to the same levels as 1986. Newspaper advertising will not capture your audience anymore – especially if your target consumer is under 54!

o Consumption of TV via DVR and Hulu or other online access eliminates most commercials – even though the average consumer still spends 8.5 hours a day watching TV, the majority of this is DVR playback which means that ads can be skipped. (Source: Nielsen & Ball State Study 2009). Hulu and other sites are growing; Hulu is now growing faster than You Tube at 13%. Hulu is now the number two website for videos. 42.4 million people used Hulu in October 2009. (Source: ComScore)

o Magazine circulations are declining – Magazines have also seen a sharp decline in circulation as well as advertising. Newsstand sales have dropped 33% from 2002-2009 and paid circulation has dropped 7.2% for the top 100 consumer magazines. (Source: Mediapost)

o Even email is starting to decline in favor of messaging through social media such as LinkedIn and Facebook, especially in the under 30 group. Email site usage has dropped from 46% to 27% between 2003 and 2009. (Source: Online Publishers Assoc).

o Some companies are starting to use Facebook as their website and there is a lot of buzz in web development circles that this is a coming trend as Facebook adds usability to the fan page.

• It is a real time CONVERSATION with your customers and consumers – this has always been the ideal for business, to know what your customers are thinking and have them tell you what they want. You no longer need to run focus groups or spend large sums of money for quantitative research. The answers are out there and your customers are only too happy to tell you what they think. Here are some things you need to remember as you get involved:

o Your consumers have an expectation of immediate information and real time conversations. Social media isn't static like traditional media and it isn't one way.

You can't just direct messages out; you have to be part of the conversation which means two-way communication and responsiveness when your customers talk to you. You have to be open to this and respond in a positive way to any feedback you receive, even if you don't like it.

o Your consumers expect to be part of your "tribe" (a Seth Godin term). Your customers will want to feel like they belong to your "club". They are looking for community and a sense of belonging; you need to provide that sense of belonging.

o Customers will share what they do and don't like about your participation so you need to monitor and be responsive. Listening is the key to being successful in social media.

• Most social media is FREE as opposed to traditional media. The cost to have someone monitor the conversation may not be totally free (someone or some department needs to own this and you may have to add staff to manage it). This makes it accessible to every size business and allows them to access new customers and consumers without any "friction" (the cost to acquire). Any business can look and act "big" on-line; a small businesses' website can look as good as the big guy, and if you have on-line commerce, there is the opportunity to sell to anyone anywhere. Plus online advertising in many industries is very inexpensive; the CPM (cost per thousand) to reach your customers can be pennies and you can control your budget in most cases by paying by view or click through. You can also advertise on Google and pay to bring up your SEO ranking (there are numerous resources that can go into this in detail) which makes you look bigger too.

• SPEED is both an advantage and critical. No one is waiting for information or response – it is all in real time, not linear like it used to be. When you send a message you need to be there to answer the immediate response you will receive. Think about the "old days" when you used mail or a messenger; you could wait days for responses! Then you had email so you could send out emails and get responses in 24 hours. Now you have Social

Media – your responses will be immediate. It allows you to get your message out in real time – and respond to questions from your customers immediately. Imagine how much more quickly you can get a new product launched and how quickly you can judge how big a hit it will be!

- Have you heard a new term called "Crowd Sourcing"? This is the ability to group source your product development, media plans and even your newsletters from blog posts. You can ask your customers to help you develop your products; ask them what media they consume or even see what your most popular blog posts are to use them for newsletters. Your customers are your best source of information to tell you what they want, how they want to hear about it and how they want to buy it. And you didn't have to pay anyone to get these answers for you. So have you asked them?

- EVERYONE in every demographic is online every day. This is now THE source for information, connecting and sharing. 60% of US Households have an internet connection according to the US Census but an even larger proportion, 72% are online (add access at work or school). Think older folks aren't online? 45% of 70-75 year olds are online today (source: Pew Group). Think about your personal habits – where do you go for information these days?

- Your customers are talking about you online whether you are there or not. Do you know what they are saying about you? And are you being honest with them? Consumers expect a high degree of transparency from companies they associate with and will call you on any behavior they find opaque or dishonest.

So how do you get started? Listen. Set up Google Alerts so you can see what is being said about your company (and your competitors). Sign up for Facebook and Twitter and see what people are doing, including people and companies in your industry. Find the people in your company who are very comfortable online and empower them to represent your company. Hire a social media monitoring firm such as Radian6. Use YouTube to show people how to use your products or share new products; give your customers a virtual tour or a glimpse into your company. Use Twitter and Facebook to connect with your customers and to be part of that conversation that may be happening with you. Then have some fun with it – it doesn't all need to be selling and business; the most successful users are those that bring in the human and let their community express themselves.

Social Media won't totally replace everything else you do to reach your customers – and it shouldn't. There is a place for traditional media, research and outreach. But not using Social Media means that you are missing a critical component of the marketing mix in reaching your customers.

Facebook, Twitter, You Tube, and other appropriate sites can make a powerful story for your company. And having a story and sharing it is the most powerful way to grow your business!

5

Taking the Mystery out of Social Media

By Lee Pound

It snuck up on us.

The Social Media revolution surprised and confounded virtually everyone in business. From being dismissed as the place where college kids chatted about nothing, it has suddenly become THE place where business owners meet clients and where deals get made.

Yet most business owners have no idea how powerful this new networking medium has become in today's world. Most of the ones I talk to have heard of it, maybe even dabbled in it and most of them agree that they just might have to learn how to use it.

Those who have tried it wonder what the fuss is all about since they often see little result and are ready to give up. If this sounds like you, gather round and let's remove the mystery.

What Social Media is and what it is not

The names seem like a blur of crazy made-up words. The process sounds bizarre. People rave about results and just as many complain about no results. Those who jump in see a bewildering array of

29

messages pass in front of them, seemingly meaningless and disconnected. The people behind these messages seem shadowy and in fact many do not even exist. This uncertainty creates an undercurrent of danger.

We'll talk about sites shortly. First, however, let's explore what social media is.

To understand it, we need to go back to the days before the Internet. People met each other at parties, mixers, networking events and at work. They met at social events, civic functions and in organizations. Virtually all the connections were local. You knew people from your community very well and knew almost nobody from anywhere else. You met the same people over and over again and got to know them well.

This system worked well. It relied on personal contact, on working with a small group of people to accomplish specific goals such as a Kiwanis Club fundraiser. However, as a means of meeting people, it was slow and restricted.

It was all we knew.

Enter the Internet with its quick connections to people all over the world. At first static web sites did most of the work. Communication was one way, from the web site to the viewer. We still met people in the same way, at parties, mixers, networking events, that is, face to face.

Then came the interactive web sites. Places where the viewer could answer back. Crude at first, they gradually grew in sophistication. Comments appeared on blogs. Then came the social networking sites. Again crude at first, they became ever more powerful means of keeping in touch.

And here's the key point. They were simply extensions of the already existing personal interaction. Facebook, for example, started as a way for friends at Harvard University to keep in touch with each other. At first, friends were actual physical friends you knew. Virtual friends came later. Connecting with people you'd never heard of came later.

Social media is a way to network, one of many. It supplements physical meetings rather than replacing them. It allows the same connection process we have always used to take place faster. And it allows us to know people better before we connect with them.

Social Media Sites Have Personalities

A key factor is that just as networking groups differ widely in nature, social media sites also vary greatly.

For example, LinkedIn is a heavily business related site. It is built around the idea that real life connections are to be encouraged and virtual ones entered into carefully. It also carefully controls access to others beyond your small circle of immediate connections, making it difficult to connect with people you have never met in person. It's almost like a table in a boardroom where you can talk to the people nearest you but any other connection is difficult. This is much like a very structured networking event.

Twitter is very different. It is more like a big networking event in which people mill about, conversations happen and anyone can listen in or join in. The big difference is that in the Twitter virtual networking arena, you can find out quite a lot about a person before you join their conversation. It is unstructured and anyone can follow or listen to anyone.

The first key to using social media correctly is to understand the personality of the various sites. Learn what their purpose is, the kinds of people they attract, and the kind of conversations that take place before you join in the conversation. The second key is to remember that social media sites are about relationships. Just as you wouldn't bring up business when you first meet someone at a party at a friend's home, you don't talk about business until you have some kind of connection.

Using Social Media for Business

As a business owner, your job is to sell yourself, your products and your services. To do this you must build relationships with your potential customers and those potential customers must be able to find you and find out about you.

In the past you put up a web site and after a while it got indexed somewhere on Google, maybe page 43, or maybe page 1. You were potentially findable if someone put in enough of the right keywords. And you got just one listing for your website.

Success on Google and other search engines comes not from having one site listed high but from having a lot of listings, at least a few of which rank high in Google.

These days Google is more interested in dynamic copy than static copy. It indexes new material more highly and more quickly than web sites that never change. This means that social media sites, including blogs, and video sites, will show up quicker and higher on Google than your traditional web site. One time I posted on my blog and checked Google a few minutes later for it. I found it already indexed.

The more places you are listed, the more places you have articles, the more social media profiles you have up, the more you are likely to come out on the first few pages of the search engines. Potential employers and potential clients will find you and go directly to your content, which shows your expertise, your location and your availability.

Getting Past Gatekeepers

In the old world of marketing, the prime emphasis was getting past the gatekeeper, that secretary who answered the phones and mail and filtered everything before it got to the boss.

In the social media world, you can contact many otherwise inaccessible people. You can even have a conversation with them, get to know them on a more personal basis, and then maybe do business with them.

Branding Yourself

Twitter and Facebook posts are primary branding tools for you as an employee and as an entrepreneur. Your posts and your profile should contain some personal information but they should be professional and show your expertise. Every time you write on the Internet, you are giving people tips, information, ways to succeed, and in general showing what you know.

For instance, on LinkedIn you can answer questions other people ask in quite a lot of detail. On Twitter and Facebook you can also answer questions, although in a shorter format.

You can also post articles on article directory sites. In many cases people will read them and comment on them and may even use them in their newsletter publications.

Finally, you can put up a blog where you discuss items where you have expertise, give new ideas, solutions and tips, and generally brand yourself as an expert in a certain area.

Conclusion

Social media started as a way for friends to communicate on the web more easily. It evolved into a powerful business tool that allows businesses to connect with clients and employees to connect with potential employers.

The rules vary from site to site. In general they follow the pattern of real life networking groups and situations.

They allow you to post large amounts of information all over the Internet so people seeking your expertise can easily find you.

Finally, social media allows you to build relationships with people you may never have met in real life because they live hundreds if not thousands of miles away.

34 Adapt or Perish

6

Strengths of a Company or Person

By Mark Fierle

Over the years a company or person either grows or they get comfortable with their place in the world. During good times they often expect that the good times will last forever. Often the company bloats or fails to invest in new products or systems.

A person frequently exhibits this when thinking, "I'm doing enough so I won't go to those night classes that will get me an advanced degree like I planned. After all I'm working 50 hours a week."

Then the inevitable comes, a downturn or the loss of motivation to improve. For a company or individual, this can result in the company going out of business, loss of a job or even worse.

Here are some ideas that may be helpful for both an organization and an individual.

Strengths of an organization
- Motivated people that are interested and take the steps to improve themselves, their products, services, and systems
- Being in the right business, filling people's needs

- Location: where needed
- Adaptable to the times, otherwise they perish

Strengths of an individual

- Open mindedness: willing to work on personal improvement all the time
- Experienced: nothing greater if we have #1
- Willing to listen: and do something about it
- Willing to put forth the effort to be successful: hours, classes, and a never satisfied attitude
- Thorough: going through the motions leaves a lot to be desired
- Motivation is the key: brains are secondary

Why is improvement important to a company or individual?

- Think about it and look at the alternatives. If we don't work on improving all the time and everyone else is, where does that leave us?
- Improving helps achieve our goals. If we reach a goal, reward yourself and set new goals. Goals are great motivators. Motivated companies and people get things done. Even if you don't quite achieve your intended goal, you will be much better off than before. Learn to incorporate goals into your everyday life. There are some great books out there on the subject. One that I like suggests developing a discipline that focuses on daily, weekly, monthly and yearly goals.
- If we don't improve ourselves or our company, who will? What have you done recently toward this end? If you can't think of much it doesn't bode well for you in today's fast paced world. I might add that this applies to all, young and old. With all the medical improvements chances are we will live a lot longer than prior generations. Why not work at improving all our life?
- Improvement is necessary for a better world. Amen. After all, where would we be if improvements stopped 20 years ago? What about my cell phone, texting, GPS, computer, HDTV and on and on. I think you get the point.

Why don't we work on improvements more?

- Not motivated. We are back to that again. Must be boring
- Not curious. As youngsters we got into everything because we were curious. As a result we learned a lot as young people. Maybe our parents' constant reprimand to stay out of this or that killed some of our curiosity. Curiosity is a gift. Let's not give it up.
- Satisfied. Enough said. Would you want a satisfied person working for you? A happy, curious, motivated person, yes. A satisfied person, no! Especially in these times.
- I'm doing enough! Man, have I heard that before. Just the kind of person that has been unemployed the past two years, living on unemployment, wondering why they can't get or keep a job. No place for improvement in this person's career life. You can always do more.
- Negative Attitude. Attitude is one of the greatest attributes or liabilities a person can have all through their life. The result can be few friends; no one wants to work with them. As an employer you have to be desperate to have them working on your team. Attitude makes up for many deficiencies. Work on it all the time.
- Not interested. What are you interested in? What will it do to make money, save money or save time for the company that is going to pay you? As an alternative, why not just get a consulting job and have them pay you to do the things you are interested in doing? Hope it works out.

Look at strengths and reasons to constantly work on improvements, goals and motivation for you as an individual and a company or organization. This will help make for a long, happy and successful career and life.

38 Adapt or Perish

7

Adapt or Perish: Resiliency Keys to Success for Individuals and Organizations

By VaNessa Vollmer, Psy.D.

Success seems to be largely a matter of hanging on after others have let go. –William Feather

Feather's advocacy of persistence evokes a poignant image of climbers holding on to or slipping off of a mountain ledge. In this context, persistence is obviously successful. However, this endorsement of persistence does not hold up as a universal admonition for success in business or personal life.

In complex real life arenas use caution as you decide what to hang on to and what to let go of. Hanging onto a toxic relationship or a failing business strategy too long can bury us in consequences so deep that our efforts to fix the situation can prevent or delay our future success.

A passenger on the Titanic would have been better off jumping empty-handed into a lifeboat rather than persistently hanging onto a treasure-filled steamer trunk. Individuals and organizations can also increase their chances of success by mentally preparing themselves before crises occur with awareness that change is the new constant in today's world and adaptation is the new constant for success.

Success seeking individuals, in both their private lives and in organizations, must operate in a paradigm where reprioritizing and adaptation become the new "Normal." When this process of adaptation becomes our daily path to success, it will give persistence a healthy role.

Our process will become easier as we realize that by analyzing problems, generating options, creative changing and ongoing evaluation; *our little steps are actually little successes.* When this process becomes mentally automatic, we will take joy and satisfaction from our daily progress rather than feeling failure and depression from striving toward rigid goals that we never quite attain.

Having a healthy approach to life and work is more important than creating a particular product! (This orientation is actually more likely to get you products.) Both personal conditions and world conditions change, and products age and wax and wane with changing fads. When you live your life by adapting and not fixating on the goal or product, you will not only become more resilient, you will become more positively motivated, more culturally successful and more personally happy.

In this chapter we will examine elements of adaptation and resiliency that help you in the pursuit of success. We will discuss and offer suggestions on the elements of:

- **What is the successful Goal?** Specify what the goal is in its purest sense of success. Make sure it is based in best practices for your industry.
- **Ongoing evaluation**, Keys to "early warning" signs of the impending need for readapting, and readapting.
  - o **Assessing our assets:** Checking and covering our abilities, resources, personal needs, etc. to exercise options.

- **What are our Assets?** Money, recognition, ideas, investors.
- **What is working?** Don't change what is working at this time.
- **What is not working?** What are the possible weaknesses?

- **Generating options**, scrutinizing the viability of hypotheses ahead of time, eliminating or reducing the costs of the **errors** in the impulsive trial and error approaches.
- **Problem analysis,** What went wrong and how to learn from our mistakes.
- **Imminent Failure Recognition:** If you are about to fail, when to persist or let go; when to cut losses and go on.
- **Enjoying success:** Suggestions for healthy, satisfying, long term life management.

While William Feather may have thought that success aligns with persistence, there is usually an obvious choice when deciding what to hang on to and what to let go of. In the case of the Titanic, the better choice was to leave the ship as it eventually sank and move on in a lifeboat or hang on to floating luggage that would support your weight. Clinging to the wreckage of something that once was great can prove fatal for some organizations. Sometimes it's more effective to adapt by releasing the wreckage and retaining the valuable lesson learned.

Which one are you?

Adaptation from one business success to the next paradigm shift is a necessary process for long term success. In order to do this, you need to respect the current success and keep your mind open to innovation as you create a shared vision and commitment for the future. There are a variety of strengths found in individuals, regions and organizations.

Survival and success depends on how well someone adapts to the changes around them. It's been said that it doesn't matter what happens to you, it's more important to handle it well. This is the path that many successful people have taken.

How do you define success? Is it being a Bill Gates, Albert Einstein, Clint Eastwood, Donald Trump, J. K. Rowling, Joe Montana, Magic Johnson, Martha Stewart, Paul McCartney, John Williams, Oprah Winfrey, or Mark Zuckerberg?

While many recognize Albert Einstein's name as the father of Relativity and other scientific contributions, few realize that after he graduated from college he had a hard time finding a job.

Einstein wanted to teach at a University. When that didn't happen, a classmate's relative helped him get a job as a patent office clerk. Einstein worked several frustrating years there. Later, he realized that some of what he learned while working there contributed to his future success and theories when his papers were published and he was eventually offered a position to teach physics.

There are assessments that differentiate people's strengths. Do you know what your strengths are? Do you leverage them for success?

I'm surprised and amazed at how many people are not aware of their strengths. Whether people are working or are in transition, ask them, "What are your strengths? What are you great at doing? What does your employer value you for in the organization?" It's amazing what you will hear. It's unfortunate that you don't hear a lot!

Unfortunately, some of the people I have met are in transition precisely because they do not know what their core strengths are. If they don't what their strengths are, how can they leverage them in business? You can't and neither can they!

Some people are in transition precisely because of this lack of knowledge and need to start somewhere. Either they didn't know their strengths or their employer didn't know their strengths. When budget time comes and positions get eliminated, what does management look at and how do they decide who stays and who they can't afford to lose? The known quantities and qualities critical to the business.

Consider different processes and assessments as you determine your personal and professional strengths and assets. At the first level it is important to remember JoHari's Window below.

This shows how we can collect information that helps us know ourselves better and how others get to know us better. The four quadrants represent the categories of awareness. The goal is to open the window panes so that we learn more about ourselves and what we share with others.

JoHari's Window	
What you know about yourself and others know about you	What you don't know about yourself and others know about you
What you know about yourself and others don't know about you	What you don't know about yourself and what others don't know about you

There are assessments for our strengths. Marcus Buckingham has written a couple of books on finding your strengths: *Now, Discover Your Strengths* and *Go Put Your Strengths to Work*. He worked with the Gallup organization, which also offers their version for assessing your strengths.

It's good for everyone to take assessments to find out what their strengths are and if they are aligned with what they are currently doing in their career. Some people are in transition because they were not aligned appropriately in their last job. It is better to find out now and re-gear to adapt wisely rather than repeat the lesson.

Career Crisis and Commitment

Usually there are four different scenarios for how people begin work and eventually end up in different careers. Many of these career issues are first considered in adolescence and emerge in adulthood.

1. Some people go into a job because their parents tell them 'this is what you're going to do' and they follow these instructions without question. For instance, parents who are doctors may expect that their child will be a Doctor too. They make a commitment without exploring other alternatives.

2. Another group struggles with decisions and is in the process of exploring different interests and needs. They explore many different directions but eventually commit to a professional career.

3. Some don't have a direction of interest nor do they have a commitment to professional goals or values. They are not

seeking options or trying to develop goals. Some people in this category become aimless drifters.

4. Another set achieves success in a certain professional direction because they actively struggled and explored several options before developing their personal professional goals.

The work of James Marcia describes these four categories of professional interest and identity development. When someone experiences job loss or other major life transitions, other processes occur in some people as described in #4 that include additional reflection and reassessment.

This fifth category occurs when someone looks at their career from a different perspective.

They assess their current:

- Needs versus wants
- Likes and dislikes about professional experiences
- Options to explore interests and leverage their experience.

With more perspective in mid-career, people may redesign their careers.

Making a decision to take the best and leave the rest results in refined career directions. Some people take this opportunity to give back to the community and teach, coach, or mentor while others explore entrepreneurial options. Others look for opportunities where they can meet professional needs and have more of a balance to meet personal family priorities.

For instance, a workaholic may reflect on their career and think about all of the social engagements that they had missed because they worked late, like dinner with friends. They might experience an illness where they take stock of the quality of their life, stress levels, time, health and resources. Both possibilities may lead to alternative professions and produce different career choices.

Assessments measuring how people handle stress in life offer additional insight for addressing health and life balance issues. People respond to stress in different ways. Some buckle under the pressure while others tough through life's challenges.

Plenty of people will tell you that you can't do something. For example, many people are familiar with the originator of FedEx, who submitted his idea in college, received a less than satisfactory grade on his paper and a comment from his instructor that, "This idea will never work." Yet he focused on his idea and made his dream a successful business reality.

Other resilient people have gone through challenging times and risen to the top. Physical disability means little in the hiring process as long as you focus on finding someone whose strengths can be of great value to the organization.

I'm familiar with a classy and dear colleague who was a drummer with two bands that toured nationally. He also recorded timeless songs such as *Unchained Melody* by the Righteous Brothers. Earlier in his musical career, he played with Dick Dale and the Deltones and was in the movie *Muscle Beach Party*. While on tour with the Righteous Brothers, he was drafted, attended officer candidate school and became a Nuclear Weapons Disposal (EOD) officer. He served in Germany, Vietnam and a number of locations in the United States.

In 1975, he left the Army, returned to college and completed his college degree. He went to work for a national CPA firm (now Ernst and Young). After three months with the firm, one evening he went out to dinner with his wife and when he returned home, had a brain hemorrhage, requiring the removal of a portion of his cerebellum. The damage created by this medical event was life changing for him. His family was concerned about his prospects for recovery.

While in the hospital, his father was telling him his concern, and Andrew heard him and could see his father's worry written all over his face. At that moment, Andrew, who was unable to talk, wrote a message for his father on a piece of paper, "I'm going to be OK," to reassure him. His (Andrew's) demonstrated resiliency comes from a strong sense of life purpose. He learned to walk and talk again and is now leading a rewarding, purposeful life. Andrew Johnson's leadership and valuable insights continue to positively impact the lives of executives who will remember his lessons for years.

As a living example, he "walks the talk!" Inner resilience like this comes from a place of hope for the future. He shares his experience and has a successful career coaching and inspiring professionals in transition. If you can get through a medical event like that, you will learn lessons that help others and that's what he does. Professionals gain realistic perspectives on life and changes in careers.

Another example of resiliency involves a person who went down in a small plane crash. He was taken to the hospital and told that he might not walk again. However, he went through several years of rehab with focused determination and re-training and now walks with crutches. Success in recovering from this type of injury depends on the amount of damage to the physical body coupled with the strength of the mindset of the individual along with the behavior they adopt to retrain their body. It helps if they have a strong belief system and effective social support system in place to encourage them through this process.

Overcoming a physical challenge in life takes determination, patience and persistence. Adaptations and insightful lessons like these are valuable to an organization, which can benefit from understanding, leveraging, and valuing such people. Anyone who can achieve dramatic results in their personal life can use similar insights and transferable strengths to overcome business challenges.

Resilient people who don't adopt a victim mentality every time something happens to them act as if adversity was a new challenge to overcome so they can thrive among us. We may never hear about some of these private champions in life or in organizations unless they share their story so we can learn from them.

Given the choice, I prefer to learn vicariously from the mistakes others make. No one needs to break their leg to know that it will hurt. You can learn from others what not to do. I saw a t-shirt that said, "Some people are great examples and others serve as warnings." I prefer to learn from success since it does not teach us what to avoid, but rather teaches us what to aspire to become.

On the other hand, revenge is a dangerous motive. However, some people are so wound up in getting revenge or justice that they are blind to logic. Critical thinking goes out the window because they are so focused on getting a result that may make them feel better. For example, in the movie *Mystic River*, directed by Clint Eastwood, Sean Penn's character wanted to hear a confession from the person who killed his daughter. Sean's character was so focused on hearing this confession that when he and the character played by Tim Robbins role played, he became emotionally caught up in the moment, and killed the wrong person. This self discipline and awareness is crucial to gain understanding, not judgment. Instead of taking inappropriate action, the person who has the patience and critical thinking skills to get to the correct answer through logic is more likely to understand.

How do we maintain a strong legacy?

The Education System and Maintaining a High Level of Knowledge

When I was in college, I had an instructor who announced to our class that we were the last of a generation who experienced education at its ultimate highest level. I asked what would happen to the generations that follow if we are the last. The instructor replied, "That's a good question. What do the rest of you think?" Over the next years, I watched the educational system decline in areas where we used to be leaders. Currently India has more honor students than the entire student population in the United States. People have advocated teaching better practical skills in school; however the need still exists for improved critical thinking skills, logic, social skills and emotional intelligence.

Government Infrastructure Supports

What does government have to do with education? The superintendent of schools supports schools. The future workers that will be hired by organizations will need to meet at least minimum standards for skills to compete in a global marketplace. If, as in the movie *The Nuremburg Trials*, Spencer Tracy's character, the judge, points out that if we stand for "justice, truth and the value of a single being" then how do we keep our educational levels where people can think in a logical manner, learn what skills it takes to do what is needed for the future generations and support a government that will deliver and encourage this in our children?

One thing I admired in our government as I was growing up was the fact that decisions were made with logical, educated thought processes. News was reported in a matter of fact manner which allowed people to form their own opinions. Decisions were made for the betterment of all human kind and we were helping others.

Other countries that acted emotionally weren't thinking things through as thoroughly, it seemed. The ones that acted out were not as strong because they were so emotionally caught up in situations. This could be completely wrong and an over simplification, however it's what I perceived as a young child.

The students of the 1960's were well educated, yet many members of this younger community rebelled, did drugs, rioted and did other short term, emotionally based and confused acts. This shift from logical processes and 1950's family values to immediate gratification and the practice of "if it feels good, do it" eventually led to awkward moments in relationships and awkward encounters later in life for those who indulged.

Individual Resiliency

Some people go through challenging situations and give up without attempting to work through them and achieve success. It is easy for some people to fail and write it off, while others leverage their spirit, stamina, strengths and determination to raise themselves successfully from the ashes. The stories we see in history and hear from around the world demonstrate humans overcoming rough and tough times. It takes determination to physically and mentally overcome damaging events like Katrina in 2005, BP's Gulf oil spill and the 9.0 earthquake in Japan.

People as individuals come together in communities to survive, overcome challenges, and thrive! The human mind and body are amazingly complex and the ability to adapt, heal, and function in response to trauma can offer insights into complex systems of excellence.

Organizational Resiliency

Organizations can modify processes to streamline production, increase productivity, make higher quality goods, and create corporate cultures that empower employees to focus and achieve unlikely yet possible goals. For example, in the 1960's when the space race was on between America and the USSR, many watched in amazement as the Russians launched the first human produced craft into space, Sputnik (translated as companion) in October 1957.

The next in the series of Sputniks, launched in November 1957, had a dog on board and was dubbed Muttnik by some. However, they didn't have a safe way to return the animal to Earth, causing the first space mission casualty. Following this loss, they launched several successful missions with plants, mice and rats aboard that were safely returned to Earth. Eventually, the Soviets successfully launched the first man into space, Yuri Gagarin, in April 1961. There were some additional successes and other failures for the Soviets; however the failures were downplayed in the controlled media.

The US continued to make progress in the space race. However, our failures were broadcast on national television. Before too much fear or concern arose, President John F. Kennedy made his famous speech that served two purposes. Fear was transformed into hope AND it gave people a visual goal: "…to land a man on the moon before the end of the decade and return him safely to Earth."

This was a goal everyone could look up at night and see in the sky, no matter where you were in the nation or in the world. Landing on the moon was the goal. It was clear and we united to make it so. From that point on, the nation supported the efforts. Scientists, researchers and engineers worked together to make the dream come true.

The Soviets backed off from going to the moon. The media reported that they didn't want to be second in anything so they wouldn't go to the moon after the Americans made it a public goal. While the Soviets may have taken the "fox and the sour grapes" attitude toward the moon, the synergy in the US propelled it forward.

This reminds me of a story about school kids going to visit the Space Center in Cape Canaveral, Florida on a day trip. The kids followed each other through the displays while they learned about space. One little girl noticed a gentleman pushing a broom in one of the large buildings. She looked around to see if anyone was watching and asked him, "Sir, what are you doing?" He looked down at the little girl, smiled and said, "I'm helping to put a man on the moon." Can you imagine the level of employee engagement when a janitor feels the mission and focused goal of his organization? Wow! *When every person throughout the organization, at every level is that clear on how their role contributes to the purpose and the ultimate goal, their behavior is aligned and the organization is effective and powerful.*

Technology and the space race focused many people on accomplishment of a goal. Another example is in the movie *The Hunt for Red October*. The US was working to keep track of new technologies in nuclear submarines so they would sneak up on Russian subs to discover systems that worked. In one scene a teacher explained, "…if we come in right behind them, in their baffles, then they are as deaf as a post." He showed why this type of stealth observation worked for gathering strategic information. Likewise, the organization that values learning, teaching, mentoring and practices transfer of knowledge behaviors will be more likely to succeed.

"Information is your friend" and the friend of the company. Collaborative work promotes success. How else would Americans ever have enjoyed Tang, the orange flavored space drink? The space program has made many discoveries that the world has benefited from.

Recently, I was talking about missed marketing opportunities with one of my friends, Stu, who is a marketing guru and worked with Ford and Kia. We were trying to remember the last time the space program budget wasn't on the chopping block. It's ironic that when the benefits of the space program were shared and marketed as a public benefit, it created interest and public awareness. The value it brought to business and the public sector was never an issue.

In more recent years, scientists, engineers and researchers continue to work on new products, including technology for health, electronics (like smart phones), and energy, but have missed many marketing opportunities.

When Lance Armstrong rode the Tour de France and ate gel with nutrients to keep up his energy, a space program product, the space program was never mentioned. Yet on NASA television, you can see presentations on 'life in space' that show how mixing the powder with liquid on earth makes things easier to eat. The astronauts could even spill a few drops of gel into weightless space and play with it, bounce it off their hands, and gulp it as it floated in space. That looks like fun!

During a recent visit to the Jet Propulsion Laboratory in Pasadena, an engineer shared some information on the importance of the quality control that goes into developing space products. If we buy something at the store that doesn't work, we can take it back and exchange it for a new one. However, if we send something into space and it doesn't work, we can't take it back for a new one. It is practical, logical and inspired technology that we as consumers ultimately benefit from. Moore's Law predicts technology improvements and facilitates continued efficiency into the 9th generation of innovation and beyond.

"Begin with the end in mind" is based on the powerful principle that all things are created twice. There's a mental or first creation, and a physical or second creation to all things, according to Stephen Covey.

What is the goal?

Start here at your goal. Plan how to finish. Plan how to run the race. Where do you need to be? Where do you start?

Ongoing Evaluation

During times of change, transition and adaptation, we need to be more aware of our social support system in our personal and professional lives because it facilitates our success through positive connections and relationships. Have positive people in your life, like other executives that have been in transition before, understand where you are, and can provide insight into what you need to do.

Enjoy Success

It is through positive connections and relationships that we support ourselves and achieve our purposes. When we experience positive connections and relationships, we are happier; we are more productive; and we are more creative.

Positive connections and relationships enhance our sense of safety and our sense of wellness. When I connect positively with others, I am more likely to take risks with what I say and how I say it, especially if I feel safe in their company. I know my audience and they know me. Success is a wonderful thing to experience and celebrate with people you have positive and healthy relationships with.

To appreciate the value of positive connections and relations, imagine not having others to relate to. My guess is that most of you would feel isolated and lonely. This perceived loneliness can happen in organizations too when there isn't an organizational process to orient, mentor and train employees. Higher engagement and retention at work includes good relationships.

Return to Ongoing Evaluation

Have a process in place to support, coach and invest in peoples' success within your organization. In some organizations, systems measure the number of hours for training on the job, in person training and online hours.

Have each region of the world tally and report training hours. This allows employees in some national or international organizations to know where they can get the most training investment. Some larger organizations have systems that allow an employee to update information on new training they received or post their interest in geographic areas where they may want to work. This information is a valuable tool when you want to retain quality people, their expertise and knowledge, and grow employee engagement.

Retention of quality employees is a key differentiator for many companies. However, during this downturn, people remember how they were treated, welcomed (or not), and followed up with during their tenure with the company.

When interested candidates apply and are left in limbo, they can be frustrated, so telling them that they are no longer being considered is closure. A "no, thanks" note is better than a warm maybe or a non-response and allows them move on to other opportunities.

Candidates who know that you need to get a certain number of "no's" before you get your 'yes' keep count so they know how much longer before they reach that 'yes.' They want helpful feedback.

When I was working to recruit people from the military I mentioned to a former service person that they should apply for a job that looked like a great fit for them. Some time went by and they called me to inquire regarding the opportunity because they couldn't find it posted on the website. When I assured them it was on the website, I looked it up and let them know it was on the fourth page of opportunities. They insisted they could only see two positions open. I went to the website, and described where the page numbers were located on the website. They asked again, "Where?" I let them know the lower left corner and described the location of the numbers in color. When there was a hesitation, I gently inquired, forgive me for asking if by chance they were colorblind. They quickly responded, "Yes!" and I asked which colors they had difficulty perceiving and they let me know.

While the colors on the website, were beautifully created to match the company logo and colors, it was designed in a way that ruled out the opportunity for people with a type of perceptual colorblindness that would have excluded key candidates with the additional skills the company was seeking due to a perceptual difference. From that point, I clarified whether this candidate could see the different web pages, but they could not. I went to the IT Director managing those who were in charge of the website and explained the problem. If we were seeking candidates with specific previous experience, then we needed to consider changing the web page colors for candidates to see the different pages of job openings. They agreed and worked the needed color changes into the web page design, so more eligible candidates could be aware of all pages listed with job openings.

When recruiting, consider the audience of possible candidates and characteristics that may hamper practicality in the process.

Some organizations will tell candidates why they were not hired. This may be gutsy but it gives candidates the information they need to understand how to improve. This approach is helpful because it lets the candidate know what others who applied for this opportunity had that they didn't and makes it less personal. Remember the "human" side for your resources.

Another option is to ask unhired candidates for referrals of people they know that might be a better fit. A company on the East Coast does this with every candidate. Each person leaves knowing why they were not hired and what the company is looking for so they learn how to professionally develop or who to refer to work there. How many of you have unhired candidates pro-actively referring candidates to your company? Consider unhired candidates enthusiastically telling others "I wasn't hired there, however they are a great organization to work with and I'm going to reapply once I have my college degree!"

If candidates don't care about their relationship to the organization, it compromises the company's mission. We can expect consequences. It is important to establish a firm pursuit of the goals of the organization and to coach each other to continuously improve.

Organizations want everyone to join together to pursue goals because just one person can sabotage the effort. If you pre-engage people at the applicant level because they want to contribute to the cause as part of your organization, it's far better than hiring applicants who just want a paycheck!

Learning about success and ongoing evaluation
The Touchstone, By Author Unknown

When the great library of Alexandria burned, the story goes, one book was saved. But it was not a valuable book; and so a poor man, who could read a little, bought it for a few coppers.

The book wasn't very interesting, but between its pages there was something very interesting indeed. It was a thin strip of vellum on which was written the secret of the "Touchstone"!

The touchstone was a small pebble that could turn any common metal into pure gold. The writing explained that it was lying among thousands and thousands of other pebbles that looked exactly like it. But the secret was this: The real stone would feel warm, while ordinary pebbles are cold.

So the man sold his few belongings, bought some simple supplies, camped out on the seashore, and began testing pebbles.

He knew that if he picked up ordinary pebbles and threw them down again because they were cold, he might pick up the same pebble hundreds of times. So, when he felt one that was cold, he threw it into the sea. He spent a whole day doing this but none of them was the touchstone. Yet he went on and on this way. Pick up a pebble. Cold - throw it into the sea. Pick up another pebble and throw it into the sea.

The days stretched into weeks and the weeks into months. One day, however, about midday, he picked up a pebble and it was warm. He threw it into the sea before he realized what he had done. He had formed such a strong habit of throwing each pebble into the sea that when the one he wanted came along, he still threw it away.

So it is with opportunity. Unless we are vigilant, it's easy to fail to recognize an opportunity in hand and it's just as easy to throw it away.

The best opportunities come when we notice a crisis and then act to turn crisis into success. Habits are actions we take without noticing. They happen over and over again. We know crises will come when we least expect them. The difference between successful and unsuccessful people is that successful people anticipate that there will be a crisis, and plan to deal with it. It becomes an opportunity to teach, mentor and learn. "Damage control" is how many people and organizations usually handle crisis. However, when you plan in advance and create strategies for when a crisis does happen, you will succeed.

I read an article that stated life crises on some level will occur about once every 3 to 5 months and can affect various areas of one's life. Knowing this in advance is a huge relief! For those who don't and who think that life is fair and believe it should be smooth sailing have two options:

1.) Consider this information and plan ahead so the effect of the next crises that comes up can be addressed with minimal impact, or

2.) Continue to get depressed every time something bad happens. This difference includes people you allow into your life as friends, partners, and the people you hire in your organization.

People come into your life for a reason, a season, or for a lifetime. Consistency and time tells you who is which. Some people understand that to have quality relationships it is important to nurture those you know. Some friends will nurture your friendship with consideration, empathy, humor and understanding and share in your ups and. These lifetime friends care about and encourage you during tough times.

Other people in your life will utilize your resources for a shorter period of time. Relationships like this occur because you have something that someone wants or needs, or you need something specific from them. Some of these relationships are mutually beneficial like a win-win. However, short term relationships can leave a person in a less than desirable position, (win-lose or lose-lose situation) especially if one of those involved has a less developed sense of ethics.

Ongoing Evaluation Revisited

Ethics in relationships show up in values, beliefs and behaviors. Some self-serving people do not understand what it might feel like to be on the receiving end of their actions. Sociopaths have no remorse.

A colleague, who was in transition, told me of their experience going to dinner with some of their friends. Since they were carefully watching their budget, they were concerned when they noticed that one or two others in the group ordered more expensive items on the menu then later asked to equally split the bill amount. They felt embarrassed because they ordered food according to what their budget was and this experience would leave them short. They didn't feel it was fair since it created an awkward situation for everyone.

The second time this happened, the same people ordered higher priced items again but again waited until the bill came to suggest splitting it equally. They were shocked at this behavior. The people seemed insensitive to the fact they were not working, yet insisted on splitting the bill equally. This time my colleague said that they were watching their budget and ordered based on that. Everyone in the party agreed to pay for what they ordered so it was resolved.

It is one thing to have this happen rarely, however if it becomes a pattern, you need to protect yourself and your budget. Watch carefully to see if you find yourself in this position rarely or more than once.

If it occurs once it's an incident, twice it's a trend and three times, it's a lifestyle. Have your contingencies to protect your budget ready in advance: Ask for a separate check or propose splitting the check before ordering so you and the group can make an informed decision.

People who call themselves friends yet treat people they know badly are not behaving as true friends. They keep you around to use you and will nickel and dime you to death (and probably not hesitate to take all the leftovers home). If you discover that you have people like this in your life, minimize time with them. Resiliency includes self-protection and mutual reciprocity in healthy relationships.

Healthy friends will reciprocate by taking turns paying the bill when you go to dinner with them or agree to payment rules in advance. Socializing with them can be far more fun, relaxing and enjoyable because you don't have to be on guard all the time and you know what to expect, healthy FUN!.

The basic foundations of trust in personal or business relationships are important for creating and maintaining longer term, respectful relationships. I like to trust people with responsibility. However, if for some reason they prove that they can't be trusted with a certain level of responsibility, then I will decide what level of responsibility I can trust them with. They may not like it. However, until they demonstrate they can handle that level of responsibility again, I won't ask them to take care of anything more important.

It is a logical process to protect yourself by remembering the 100/0% rule. Take 100% responsibility and expect nothing in return; however the dynamics of that relationship change. Be careful of those who are not ready, willing, or able to have that same level of mutual respect and responsibility. If they work on it and develop and demonstrate better responsibility behaviors, it may be appropriate to eventually trust them with gradually increasing levels of responsibility after learning additional skills. Determine the level of responsibility they can successfully handle and go with that in the interim. It will be more comfortable for future interactions.

Assessing our Assets and Success

The story of the frog and the scorpion is a timeless lesson. It differentiates between those who want and ask for help to genuinely improve themselves in personal or professional development versus those who want to take advantage because it's their nature.

The Scorpion and the Frog

A scorpion climbed over rocks until he reached a river. The river was wide and swift, and the scorpion stopped to reconsider the situation. He couldn't see any way across. He saw a frog sitting by the bank of the stream. He asked the frog for help to get across the stream. "Would you give me a ride on your back across the river?"

"Mr. Scorpion! How do I know that if I try to help you, you won't try to *kill* me?" asked the frog hesitantly.

"Because," the scorpion replied, "If I try to kill you, then I would die too, since I cannot swim!"

Now this seemed to make sense to the frog. But he asked. "What about when I get close to the bank? You could still try to kill me and get back to the shore!"

"This is true," agreed the scorpion, "But then I wouldn't be able to get to the other side of the river!"

"How do I know you won't just wait till we get to the other side and THEN kill me?" said the frog.

"Ahh...," crooned the scorpion, "Because once you've taken me to the other side of this river, I will be grateful for your help. It would hardly be fair to reward you with death, would it?!"

The frog agreed to take the scorpion across the river. He swam over to pick up his passenger. The scorpion crawled onto the frog's back, his sharp claws prickling into the frog's soft skin, and the frog slid into the river. The frog stayed near the surface so the scorpion would not drown. He kicked strongly against the current.

Halfway across the river, the frog suddenly felt a sharp sting in his back. Out of the corner of his eye, he saw the scorpion remove his stinger from his back. A deadening numbness crept into his limbs.

"You fool!" the frog croaked. "Now we will both die! Why on earth did you do that?" The scorpion shrugged, and did a little jig on the drowning frog's back. "I could not help myself. It is my nature." They both sank into the muddy waters of the swiftly flowing river.

It is important to identify who is like frogs in contrast to self destructive behavior that stings or kills like the scorpion in this story.

This identification process applies in your personal life and within your organization. If you have a frog with the gift of swimming and transporting the scorpion to the other side of the river, why not protect the frog from the scorpion whose nature it is to hurt others even to their own detriment? Sociopaths or people in strong denial can affect relationships in business and in personal lives. Stinging the frog halfway across the river does no one any good.

Frogs are usually not noticed in the environment except on a noisy Spring night near water, a shadow on a leaf, or found in a moist place discovered in the yard, yet they appear when you need them to help eat what bugs you in life.

Protect the frogs in your life and your organization. They will help deal with what bugs you so you can enjoy life more.

- Friends
- Responsible and reciprocal
- Outstanding and optimistic
- Genuinely grounded
- Social support system and sounding board.

Frogs are quality colleagues and long term friends. They will be there for you down the road when you need them. Likewise, they will reciprocally reach out when they need you to be a frog for them.

Pick your employees wisely, select high quality friends, and you will surround yourself with a healthy ecosystem in work and life.

One learns to adapt to the land in which one lives. ~Louis L'Amour

References:
Bovet, David and Martha, Joseph (2000). *Value Nets: Breaking the Supply Chain to Unlock Hidden Profits*
Buckingham, Marcus. *Now, Discover Your Strengths* (2011). *Go Put Your Strengths to Work!* (2007)
Covey, Steven (2003). *The 7 Habits of Highly Effective People*
Froschheiser, Lee; Chutkow, Paul and Kemp, Barry. (2006) *Vital Factors: The Secret to Transforming Your Business - and Your Life.*
Sartain, Libby and Schuman, Mark, (2006). *Brand From The Inside: Eight Essentials to Emotionally Connect Your Employees*
Stout, Martha (2005). *The Sociopath Next Door*
Tichy, Noel and Bennis, Warren (2007) *Judgment: How Winning Leaders Make Good Calls*

8

Being Outrageous to Succeed

By Steve Amos

It is not enough to be good at your job. There are plenty of people who are excellent at doing their jobs. Why do they get passed over when new opportunities are available? It's because the decision maker doesn't think of them as right for the opportunity.

The phrase "Adapt or Perish" has more meaning today than it ever has. If your superiors don't see you working well, they may not think of you when the time comes to promote. They may think of someone else first. Why? Perhaps because they don't know you or perhaps the timing is wrong. They did not need someone yesterday. The previous person only left today. What other reasons can you think of?

Your company cannot thrive by selling only "me too" products. Being the low cost provider is not a sustainable market position. You have to make enough profit to invest for future growth and save enough to survive down markets. Thin margins do not create sustainable businesses, except in need categories like grocery stores, which survive on 3% - 5% profit margins because everyone has to eat. But not everyone has to buy your product or service.

For you to be successful, decision makers have to choose your products and services. Remember, it is not huge corporations or government making the choice; it is a real person working for the corporation or government who makes the decision. Business is always about marketing and selling directly to people.

Do you need more proof about the need to be known?

The one factor which separates millionaire business owners from the rest is their willingness to promote themselves. Too many entrepreneurs hide behind a corporate façade, trying to make it look as if they have big corporations. People want to buy from people.

Wendy's was Dave Thomas' business. There was no fancy name picking committee. Wendy was Dave's daughter. When business needed to pick up, the leader had to speak to the customer. Dave was not a professional television spokesperson. In fact he was terrible to start. Ads had to be shot over and over again until they were good enough. But his message came through. We cook better food for you. It wasn't square hamburger patties that made Wendy's the number three burger chain, it was that you knew they were cooking good food from recipes that Dave made. And we knew Dave cared about the taste and quality of the food Wendy's served.

Donald Trump is well known for firing people on the television show *The Apprentice* today. But he was known in New York City real estate development circles many years ago. He grew up in his father's real estate business. At one dedication they introduced the man responsible for building a certain bridge. Donald realized that nobody would remember this gentleman in a few years. He determined that every project would have the Trump name on it. Donald worked hard and was known as someone who could arrange financing and negotiate with city regulators, both very valuable skills in real estate. So Donald became famous for writing about his strengths in his book, *The Art of the Deal*. This allowed "The Donald" to get better properties in New York because people would work with this young man to make money. Look at how many Trump properties are located in New York and New Jersey.

Sometimes leaders are found through crisis. Chrysler was in deep financial trouble in the 1980s. Lee Iacocca had to lead Chrysler through a government loan, bad publicity, corporate system problems, and a lack of respect. One of the most memorable parts of the recovery was when Chrysler introduced new cars and trucks that were very competitive. To overcome the poor perception of Chrysler, Lee Iacocca became the spokesman for his company. He talked about how

Chrysler had changed and become better. But I can still recall his ads telling people, "If You Can Find a Better Car, Buy It!" We heard the confidence in his people and products, and we bought. This crisis forced Lee Iacocca to stand up and be noticed as a leader.

What holds true for Dave Thomas, Lee Iacocca and Donald Trump also holds true for you. You may be shy, feel you aren't worthy, or have been trained to be humble. All of that is fine — but not in business. In business, you will get paid to the extent you are willing to promote yourself.

You earn new customers by telling the world your products and services are the best and doing business with you is the most pleasurable and worthwhile experience the customer can have. You will make a profit to the extent that you raise prices and encourage customers to compete with each other in order to have the privilege of doing business with you. All of this will come to you only if you are unabashed, only if you suppress fear and promote yourself.

Maybe the message has already hit the younger generation. Look at reality shows and all the people now famous for being famous. This generation wants to be known for something, even if most of us think it is fame for doing something embarrassing or foolish. They want their "fifteen minutes."

The good news is that you get to choose how you are noticed. You don't have to be a reality star, just be more active in groups and networks. Find mentors and volunteer to make a difference in whatever activities you participate in. Don't just sit there, do something to help. This will get you noticed.

Learn to make presentations, write articles or blog about your industry, business, hobby or passion. Make an effort to help others improve. People who do this are perceived to be experts in their field and industry. They get known by the decision makers and when opportunities happen they get the first call. Wouldn't you like your choice of opportunities?

How do you brand yourself? Pick out your natural talents and interests. Pick the part of your business you are interested in. This already puts you at an advantage. You will be more motivated to learn more and work longer than competitors who don't care. Best of all you will work using your strengths, not your weaknesses.

Today's questions are: What do you want to be known for? What are your best gifts? Join Toastmasters and speak up. Write articles for your business publications. Go to association meetings and volunteer for work that matters. Get known for doing something good and opportunities will come to you.

9

Generation Trends in the Workforce

by VaNessa Vollmer, Psy.D.

Why are generational issues important to business?

Most people have common needs. However, each generation acts and works differently. These differences create marketing segments for businesses. They also affect the way business implements best practices.

Generational differences are reflected in demographic and psychographic information businesses collect and use to market themselves. Demographics is data on populations used in sociology, public policy and marketing. Psychographics is the study of personality, values, lifestyles and culture.

While it is easy to lump people into specific generations, watch out for generalizations that do not reflect the unique differences between people. The guidelines presented in this chapter are useful as general categories. However, remember that in any generation you will find overlapping values and interests that are not generation specific.

Lifespan affects current social and business trends. Many people live longer due to better health care, nutrition, and health awareness.

Consider the difference in lifespan between 1900 to 2000, just 100 years:

- 1900 - 47 years
- 2000 - 76.5 years

As lifespan increases, the workforce adapts. This trend impacts business in a number of ways.

First, there is a serious mismatch between the skills needed in the workforce and the skills new employees bring to the workplace. Many students do not graduate from high school. Fewer students attend college and even fewer graduate. Companies must implement training programs to rectify this.

Second, current employees are fewer in number. Some are older and others are less qualified. One trend is toward younger employees taking less responsibility for the transfer of leadership roles, a global problem. Unfortunately, because companies don't react quickly to these urgent signals, transfer of knowledge becomes a problem.

Third, a recent phenomenon among what we now call "Generation Unretired" affects business as well. Many people who were retired have returned to the workforce for various reasons. For instance, health care related areas are growing fast, creating a high demand for services even as the number of qualified workers declines. Healthcare position can't be outsourced since they service local health needs while manufacturing and management jobs have been outsourced. Another trend is that more retirement-eligible workers postpone retirement because of the current recession.

Recent Retirement Changes

Eight out of ten Americans of retirement age will continue to work part or full time, according to the American Association of Retired Persons, which says that 93% of the growth in the American workforce through 2016 will come from this group. This is the largest such change in retirement since World War II (Pew Research Group).

Recent Retirees

Many recent retirees are talented, innovative, and energetic. They are sharpening their technology skills, updating resumes, scouring job boards, and re-entering the workforce. Some have personality traits that have caused challenges for business in the past, particularly in areas like transfer of knowledge and technology changes. While many lament the passing of the "way we used to do business," industries know that the challenge of competing in the global marketplace demands adaptation on many levels.

What Happened?

Different factors explain this change in un-retirement trends. Some recent retirees can't afford to stay retired since their savings were devastated by the recent market crash. This crash, coupled with the housing bubble, left many people unable to sell their homes, making them unable to access their equity and move to less expensive retirement locations. In some cases, where a family needs two incomes or has health issues, people have lost homes they owned for longer than 20 years. A much smaller number lost homes they purchased during the real estate peak in 2005-2006.

Record unemployment rates makes reentering the workforce more challenging. Many executives and managers who lost jobs due to necessary business decisions need their spouses to return to work to contribute to the household income. Many of these executives have also considered going into business. However, the costs associated with this can create challenges for the unprepared or uninformed.

Retirement has always included the need to find new interests such as hobbies and community involvement or face boredom. Many retirees participate in and contribute to their communities as part of their legacy. Others find that going back to work or starting a business is the best way to continue to grow.

What can we do to support our business?

Companies need to address five areas to ensure adaptive success:

- **Understand business trends and cycles** that are critical for investment, strategy, and planning purposes on a global basis.
- **Understand generational values** because each generation in the workforce has experienced different life events and holds different work values.
- **Encourage employee engagement** to build a connected corporate culture. Research shows that the higher the level of employee engagement, the better the business results.

- **Leverage strengths in teams** whenever possible to build a synergistic effect to complete projects and develop programs and products.
- **Identify skill gaps and develop talent.** Support processes to identify skill gaps and do succession planning with timelines, key candidates for specific roles, and leadership.

These processes will facilitate transfer of knowledge so that the business may succeed in the long term.

Long-term Generational and Financial Cycles

Some events may seem random. However, if you watch long enough, you will see a cycle of trends.

Typically, generations last about 20 to 25 years. When we apply this to average life spans, we get four stages:

- Childhood
- Young adulthood
- Midlife
- Senior years

When considering business trends, studies of different generations and how they relate to business and financial investment cycles have revealed four generational themes, according to research by Casey N. Howe and W. Strauss.

Their cycles, shown below, include the current four generations now in the workforce, two earlier generations, and one to follow.

Year Range	Nick Name	Size	Archetype
1883 – 1900	Lost Generation		(Nomad)
1901 – 1924	Waning GI's		(Hero)
1925 – 1942	Silent Gen	75 Million	(Artist)+
1943 – 1960	Baby Boomers	85 Million	(Prophet)
1961 – 1981	Gen X	46 Million	(Nomad)
1982 – 2003	Millennials (Gen Y)	76 Million	(Hero)
2004 – after	Gen Z		(Artist)*

+Tend to have risk averse, pro-conformity mindset that influences business decisions, according to the research of Casey N. Howe and W. Strauss.

*Will continue to grow in size due to US immigration.

The next section will give a brief description of these groups with ideas and insights into each generation and patterns you can expect based their life experiences.

1982 – 2003 Millennials (Waning GI's retired) (Hero Archetype)

- Protectively raised as **children**
- As **young adults** help solve a societal crisis.
- **Midlife** – institutionally powerful
- Greeted in **senior years** by uprising of a young prophet generation.
- Examples include heroes of the American Revolution.

Gen Z 2004-current & Silent Generation (1925 – 1942) (Artist)*

- **Children** of the crisis (ex. Post WWII, post financial meltdown of 2008) urgency/history change.
- As **young adults** at post-crisis era. Conformity seems best for success and risk averse.
- **Midlife**: views self as having the expertise and refinement to improve institutions and create innovation. Cultural awakening, life speeds forward as culture transforms.
- **Seniors** currently moving into gated communities (flexible elders, focused on the needs of others, elder advisors.)

1943-1960 Baby Boomers 'Generation Un-Retired' (<u>Prophet</u>)

- **Childhood:** Post crisis affluence (post American high)
- As **young adults** they go through a period of upheaval (consciousness revolution of the 60's-70's)
- **Midlife:** become moralistic and values-obsessed leaders and parents.
- During their **senior years** they experience the next great outer-world social or political crisis.

1961-1981 Generation X (Nomad)

- **Children** of an awakening and great cultural upheaval. They are usually under-protected. Learn early not to trust basic institutions to look out for their best interests.
- As **young adults** they become free agents who focus on individualism.
- **Midlife**: Great realists and pragmatists in our national history. Tend to forge their identity and value system by "going it alone" and usually don't have a strong connection to public life. *Gen X is the 1st generation to be affected by birth control.
- **Seniors** it will be interesting to watch this generation, especially in leadership roles. As parents, they are more protective because they want to offer their children protection they didn't have growing up.

Using these guidelines, watch for the interaction between the generations and the different values that the individuals have as they function in a business environment.

Generational differences infuse corporate culture. Some companies have found that Gen X and Gen Y pair well in the computer industry, where corporate culture is very different from traditional manufacturing. Some organizations in this market use different incentives to engage employees. However, given that change is constant for businesses and individuals, they will need to monitor this carefully.

For younger employees, coming of age and adapting to changes in life, business and relationships is a search for uniqueness that powers generations as they grow. People participate in business in different ways. Some go along with policies and procedures and others rebel against them.

Eventually, this discovery process leads to the realization that doing the opposite of what you are told does not define who you are and it is usually somewhere in the middle. They discover that such simplistic reactions don't define them or the organization. What once seemed liberating now limits success unless they realize this!

This quest for perspective and enlightenment requires greater understanding of corporate functions, which masterminds and mentors can provide. Younger employees benefit from the mentor's experience and seasoned mentors benefit from the younger generations knowledge of technology advances, among other things.

Connect Generations through Company Culture

Encourage employee engagement to build a connected corporate culture. The three layers of culture are:

1. Most visible and simplest: logos, colors, dress codes, the look
2. Company norms: formal and informal policies to get things done.
3. Beliefs and core values like "Customers first!"

Technology Integration – Generations Launch and Learn!

- **Selection of technology** is critical to support business infrastructure. Ease of implementation is critical to processes that serve internal and external customers and create profits. Reward current practices through effective communication. Verify that you have the systems in place to support the processes before full implementation. Test, retest and work the bugs out before the system goes live for everyone.

  Training, technology, work processes, collaboration, and communication skills work together in a system. Find out what works and what helps ease workflow, which makes everyone's life easier as part of the team. What company wouldn't want to have less grief, more productivity, and higher employee engagement? If you see an employee of one generation using *IM (Instant Messaging) on their computer, find out how or why they use it. If you find out that they have other people who help them solve work issues and they're not on your payroll, this can be helpful, however you want to be sure that compliance/security/intellectual property issues are respected. *Do the benefits of these resources outweigh the risks? Inform stakeholders and implement processes to appropriately adapt.

- **Measure and Reward:** quantify results and acknowledge great results in a manner that the person appreciates. It takes extra effort to find out what the person prefers so don't assume that you know what is best or decide for them. Invest the time to understand what motivates your employees through casual inquiry or a feedback survey.

- **Communicate shared values** in a newsletter or by intranet.
- **Legends and Folklore:** What makes your organization special? If you have a story that showcases success in the organization, make sure everyone knows it, can tell the story, and understands its importance! These are stories you want others to emulate in your organization.
- **Role models are important** for socialization. As people are oriented to the company they learn what the company looks for and what rewards it gives. Demonstrate that certain contributions are valuable to the organization based on values, priorities and commitments that return value to the bottom line.

A sense of what matters most

In contrast to the popular image of twenty- and thirty-something's returning to traditional methods, most young people want to balance work and life in the context of an equal relationship. Young adults from all economic and ethnic backgrounds generally share these egalitarian aspirations (Data from Kathleen Gerson's Research) include:

- Best practices in succession management
- Best systems that are development oriented rather than replacement oriented.
- Highly effective systems involve high level executives as a strategic tool to attract and retain.
- Identify gaps in talent.
- Identify talent early
- Constantly reinvent, refine, and adjust systems with feedback.

Succession Success!

- Succession is an organization-wide resource.
- Reliable systems to find, develop, and retain top talent.
- Support from the top is required for the best results in any organization.
- Integration of leadership development processes with successful outcomes.

- Use performance data, involve closest co-workers, build from the bottom up, invest time, and make consensus decisions.

Defining and Identifying Talent Checklist

Competency models and alignment with corporate performance objectives:

- Can include 360-degree feedback for clear expectations
- Link development to goals.
- Motivate employees to improve by offering specific guidelines.
- Set expectations for development targets.

Global Competencies

- Initiative and innovation
- Interpersonal effectiveness
- Leadership and learning
- Market focus, teamwork

Leadership Behaviors

- Model the values
- Create external focus
- Anticipate change
- Implement quality

Leadership Competencies

- Visionary
- Effective communication
- Decisiveness and follow-through
- Linking succession to development

Succession Planning for Generational Success

Focus on critical positions. "Rank and yank" doesn't work. Coaching and mentoring are very effective. Companies clearly benefit when they partner with their employees. Ensure smooth transitions by training and sharing information that enables them to succeed. Match the "right" developmental assignments with new positions.

Even though performance appraisals are subjective, begin with the desired behavior and then provide specific meaningful appraisal and feedback. Remember that just because you know what you want, you may not be able to explain it to others. Remain open to clarification.

Keep more than one qualified person in mind and groom them all because people move and life situations change. This protects the company and its future internal resources.

Higher Engagement with Higher Stock Prices

Understand engagement strategy and economic impact. When every employee wants to help the organization succeed, they have more impact than those who just come to work for a paycheck. You will get two different kinds of performance from these two different mindsets. The organization can share this knowledge with employees so that they understand what they can do to improve the company for everyone.

Customer relations, program management, human resources, contract management, engineering, and information technology are some of the departments where employees can make a difference when they understand how their roles fit into the organization as a whole. Leadership asks for and implements those items needed for successful engagement.

- Resources: Does every employee have what they need?
- Motivation: What motivates me?
- Values: Does this organization value the same things?
- Customers, employees and prospective employees will ask, "Do the values of the organization resonate with me?"

People who understand their purpose and vision can weather any storm!

Consider this an opportunity to do analysis of cohorts. Look at different coping styles and whether there is proactive leadership or crisis management with non action defaults as results.

Team dynamics can be described and leverage strengths and cross training whether it is leadership, management skills or technical skills. Foster a sense of learning in your teams and when possible your organization.

People defer to a strong leader who has optimism, a clear vision and can communicate their vision. Leadership from any generation must ensure that values, beliefs and actions align with purpose and environmental reality within the organization. One of the ways to foster this includes creating an environment of inquiry.

Different communication styles can create friction. However, if you ask questions to understand rather than to give a quick judgment that is often only partially informed, you can create a culture that is more tolerant of differences. The beneficial result is that you'll avoid communication and cultural crises while supporting people known for specific strengths, expertise and can help in those areas when needed.

Leadership and Trends

Leaders' messages in organizations need to include empathy and understanding to meet business goals. Leadership messages should avoid victim mentalities. Some people get negative attention by emphasizing every negative in their life, which distracts and is unproductive. Transforming challenges into overcoming difficulties with a focus on victories is far more healthy and productive.

Leaders who understand how to leverage organizational leadership will see the larger picture and will understand what individuals and groups need to achieve goals.

What can you expect for current retirement?

- 34% will never retire. They will do consulting, full or part time work.
- Global growth statistics: recruit locally first.

Build lateral moves within the organization to engage employees, retain interest through broadening their experiences which adds value to the organization. Some organizations promote internal "mobility programs" to facilitate employee understanding of the larger picture and cross pollinate knowledge.

Engage your employees' hearts and minds and build professional development into your organization's culture. There is an expected value when an employee comes to work in exchange for a paycheck. If you transform the employee into one that is motivated, understands their strengths and those of their team members, the value and benefits only increase!

When you have an employee who uses newer technology to get their job done more effectively, that is fine, however when they can teach others the impact on other employees of understanding these tools, use them more frequently and effectively to capture that success and build it into your bottom line!

General Generational Guidelines:

Millennials tend to prefer feedback and mentoring and are sponges for knowledge. They want the balance in life/work and are more likely to request accommodations to support these values.

Gen X will benefit from partnering with others rather than going it alone as many may be used to.

Baby Boomers' need for information will benefit them so they can make informed decisions so bring them data.

Older generations may have a different style and need to be involved in the newer processes. Invite them to contribute concerns upfront about what they

1) like,
2) are concerned about and
3) what they are willing to contribute to improve newer processes.

Remember to consider each person as an individual in each generation because each person has different learning styles, Visual, Auditory, Kinesthetic or a combination thereof. Technology interests include ALL generations. The myth of younger generation's exclusive interest in technology is not supported in research. The research shows technology interests include all generations and a rapid growing number of people adapting to social media platforms.

Strengths are the key in clarifying who does what tasks best on the team. As long as you maintain a respectful relationship environment and focus on positive outcomes, you are more likely to get it from everyone. Be sure everyone knows each other's strengths for optimal generational teamwork and celebrate it!

Generational Success Factors to Address and Implement

- Understand business trends and cycles.
- Understand generational values and strengths to build your organization, including cultural competency

- Encourage employee engagement to build a connected corporate culture.
- Leverage strengths in teams.
- Identify skill gaps and develop talent. Merge technology trends.
- Deal with health and safety issues and guide people into appropriate opportunities.

Understand the values at an individual level for each member of your team or workforce. Focus on leveraging strengths, interests in professional development, and results for multi-generational success.

References:

Bovet, David and Martha, Joseph (2000). *Value Nets: Breaking the Supply Chain to Unlock Hidden Profits*

Brower, Joseph and Gilbert, Clark. *How Managers' Everyday Decisions Create - or Destroy - Your Company's Strategy* (Harvard Business Review)

Gerson, Kathleen (2009). *The Unfinished Revolution: How a Generation is Reshaping Family, Work and Gender in America*

Howe, Neil and Strauss, William. *The Next 20 Years: How Customer and Workforce Attitudes Will Evolve* (Harvard Business Review)

Johnson, Meagan and Johnson, Larry (2010). *Generation Inc.: From Boomers to Linksters Managing the Friction between Generations at Work*

Lancaster, Lynne and Stillman, David (2010). *The M Factor: How the Millennial Generation is Rocking the Work Place*

Strauss, William and Howe, Neil (1997). *The Fourth Turning: An American Prophecy*

Strauss, William and Howe, Neil (2000). *Millennial's Rising: The Next Great Generation*

Walker, Douglas and Sorkin, Stephen. *A-ha! Performance: Building and Managing a Self-Motivated Workforce*

People are lucky and unlucky…according to the ratio between what they get and what they have been led to expect. ~Bertrand Russell

76 Adapt or Perish

10

Human Resources Professionals as Coaches:

Becoming a Strategic Partner within the Organization

By Emily Woodman-Nance

Human resource management is described as "the policies, practices, and systems that influence employees' behavior, attitudes, and performance." [1] The human resources department is critical to the advancement of an organization. When a company is equipped with a good one it will flourish.

Major trends will affect the future of business, the role of HR and will require an organization to take a different view of success. Some of these trends affecting HR are globalization, technology, diversity, sending jobs offshore, inter-generational workforce, trained workforce availability, organizational strategy and HR outsourcing. These trends impact workforce management and business development. In response to these trends, the human resources professional is becoming a strategic partner in an organization.

With the increasing role of HR, CEOs have broadened their expectations of HR. CEOs want the following from HR:

- Trusted adviser
- Great communicator
- Leader
- Cultural leader
- Outsourcing innovator
- Financial know-how
- Talent manager
- Technological wiz
- Results-driven operator
- Mergers and acquisition analyst
- Political savvy

New HR Coaching Role

To be a successful strategic partner, the human resources professional needs to determine where the organization is headed and guide the way. Coaching is a process proven to bring about organizational success. According to a study by the Manchester Group[2], organizational benefits from coaching include:

Improved Relationships	77%
Improved Teamwork	67%
Improved Job Satisfaction	61%
Improved Productivity	53%
Improved Quality	48%
Increased Organizational Strength	48%
Increased Organizational Commitment	44%
Increased Bottom Line Profitability	22%

Coaching is a creative process that inspires a person to maximize their personal and professional potential. Coaches are trained to listen, observe and customize their approach to individual client needs. They elicit solutions and strategies from the client. They believe the client is naturally creative and resourceful. The coach's job is to provide support to enhance the skills, resources, and creativity that the client already possesses and to establish accountability.

With the evolving role of HR comes the opportunity for human resources professionals to take on a coaching role. One of the most important factors the HR coach brings to this role is knowledge of the organization and the impact of the managers within that environment. The HR coach may work with every manager and supervisor at every level in the organization and focus specifically on maximizing their performance to help reach organizational and personal goals. In the capacity as coach, the HR coach would do everything from active listening to providing assessment results through establishing accountability.

When is Coaching Appropriate?

The HR coach aims to inspire company leaders and employees to take personal responsibility in the success of the organization. To reach this goal, coaching is appropriate in the following areas:

- Maximizing management and leadership potential
- Developing and maximizing global leadership
- Employee development
- Formal succession planning
- Communication
- Assimilating a new employee ("on-boarding")
- Goal-setting
- Time management
- Taking charge of a job transition within the organization
- Developing effective working relationships within the organization

Coaching Paired With Training

"A study featured in *Public Personnel Management Journal* reports that 31 managers that underwent a managerial training program showed an increased productivity of 22.4%. However, a second group was provided coaching following the training process and their productivity increased 88%. Research does demonstrate that one-on-one executive coaching is of value." [3]

"Xerox Corporation carried out several studies on coaching. They determined that in the absence of follow-up coaching to their training classes, 87% of the skills the program brought about were lost." [4]

The new role as HR coach has the potential to revolutionize the Human Resources relationship with organization managers and executives. It will position the human resources professional as a member of the management team and will make HR successful in the future and facilitate business growth and prosperity.

Preparing HR for the new "coach" role?

To prepare for the new role as a coach in the organization, HR has to acquire a new set of competencies. Coaching presence is an integral competency. It unlocks the door to the other core competencies. The International Coach Federation defines coaching presence as follows:

"Ability to be fully conscious and create spontaneous relationships with the client, employing a style that is open, flexible and confident."

If you are not fully conscious, how can you communicate effectively, facilitate learning and results, or build rapport with an employee.

The International Coach Federation and SHRM can provide an understanding of what is required to be successful in this new role as coach.

References:

[1] Noe, R., Hollenbeck, J., Gerhert, B., Wright, P. (2003). *Fundamentals of human resource management, 1e.* McGraw-Hill Companies

[2] Human Resource Executive magazine (November 2005), *What CEO'S Want: The 10 most sought-after talents of HR leaders*

[3] The Manchester Review • 2001 • Volume 6 • Number 1

[4] F. Turner, Ph.D. CEO Refresher 2001

[5] Business Wire, July 30, 2001

11

Training by Tribal Knowledge: Do's and Don'ts

By VaNessa Vollmer, Psy.D.

Tribal Knowledge refers to the vast amount of information that is unwritten yet known to a person or knowledge worker. Tribal knowledge can specifically refer to a person's in-depth knowledge about a specific project or process. In some cases, a person may be considered a subject matter expert.

Tribal knowledge is important and is a challenge to teach others. In fact some organizations are deeply rooted in the belief that it would be a WOMBAT (Waste of Money, Brains and Time) to ramp others up to an experienced employee's level so they keep that employee at work and miss the opportunity to facilitate a critical transfer of knowledge.

Unfortunately, many companies may not realize that they need to foster professional development through learning processes like mentoring, cross-training and documentation. The transfer of tribal information allows the company and its employees to continue to succeed in the long run. Some companies don't discover this until it's too late.

Talented workers who have been employed for years can retire, leave to go to another company or, in the worst case, get hit by a delivery truck. Think about how that immediate absence of knowledge can impact an organization.

How organizations handle tribal knowledge training

Some organizations give formal on the job training, which includes a transfer of knowledge that incorporates expertise, leverages education and facilitates a smooth transition from new hire to productive employee.

This formal training process includes a way to assess how well the new employee is learning and adapting to the new job functions. Companies can measure return on investment for this training by looking at time on the job versus time taken to attain those competencies and return productivity, time and money savings to normal levels.

Other organizations train through exposure to "on the job" situations. This approach is based on the fact that the more you perform your duties, the more you will learn. Some of these companies train employees in safety and other required items but they don't have a formal training manual or reference for employees to utilize as a source for information in their everyday duties. Employees learn by asking questions and by personal experience on the job.

Why is this important? Does it matter if the organization has a formal training process for employees? What are the 'Pros and Cons' of having a "Proactive Resource" organization or a "Reactive Resource" organization? What is it like for employees to work in these types of organizations?

These are great questions. Some companies consider having no written training program and having employees learn as they go and learn at their own speed with no specified measure of performance as a "pro." However, it will take a lot longer to transfer knowledge and train employees this way because employees learn only when a new situation presents itself. These situations may occur randomly and without warning. As a result, experienced employees will need to handle the situation or teach the new employee how to deal with it under pressure and time constraints.

Employee Experience Scenario

Let's consider what it might be like for an employee to work with a system where everything is self taught or occasionally guided by others who have more experience.

If someone says, "You should know that by now," it puts the individual at a disadvantage because there is no "by now" or timeline to learn specific tasks. This means the employee has an indefinite training period. New employees never quite know when they've learned everything or attained mastery of the job.

The new employee's feeling of continuously being in limbo makes them feel unsure of where they stand until a supervisor tells them whether they are doing a good job or not, which doesn't always happen. This keeps the new employee either ultra conscientious or paranoid. Employees need to focus on what they know. The worst case is that they are never sure where they stand and focus on their own learning process and skill attainment goals. When another new employee asks for help or training, they may say to themselves, "Nobody helped me out. I had to learn it on my own. Why help this person learn?" This method may create subtle competition with co-workers.

If you have employees who don't share a vision but are more focused on themselves as individuals because they had to self-train and figure out processes on their own, it makes a group that is:

- Individually focused on "what's good for me," not team oriented
- Competitive, with a process that discounts information from co-workers because if it is not correct it will make them look bad if things don't work out
- Resistant to collaboration that hesitates to teach and streamline operations but focuses on individual achievement.

This process results in wasted time and duplication of labor in complex problem solving. People won't listen to anyone else because they believe that they have to figure it out for themselves. That's the training model. This can result in multiple agendas for each person. Some may overlap, but many others don't. There is no unifying goal that the group can share as a team. This is more like parallel processing.

In organizations, one size does not fit all!

If you hire an engineering company to design a project, contractors to build it, set a completion deadline, and create a budget, you may still not get a fully functional product ready to put online without a lot of remedial work.

One cause is a lack of communication and oversight on the project. You might install a big assembly line upgrade and the computer program that automates it. However, if the new computer program can't run the upgraded system, you've made a costly mistake. It's like building an automated system to build domestic cars. If you create a remote control software system designed to construct a Ferrari, you can't make domestic cars. The new system requires not one but several adjustments to make it work.

Why didn't somebody notice that they were getting the wrong software system? Some people tend to oversimplify and therefore miss critical information. Unfortunately, this oversight can cost everyone time, money, and grief. The error impacts employees, customers, customers of customers and stakeholders, including the local and, in some cases, the worldwide community.

Seth Godin, in his book *Linchpin*, discusses what he calls "the resistance" to change and innovation. Each person who can do an average job gets paid to produce or gets terminated.

Some individuals in organizations are outliers because they see unique, creative ways to facilitate the company's success. Godin calls this person the linchpin. Everyone who has this creative urge has the ability to synthesize information, find solutions and bridge innovative gaps. However the resistance mentioned above tries to squeeze the creativity out of the linchpin. Organizations would prefer to have the creative part of your brain idle rather than function and scare the fearful peers that do as management asks.

Godin further shows that we are rapidly approaching the point where we can come up with unique options known as art. We are now in a race to make average stuff for average people cheaply. Producing an average idea takes little time. What's left is to take the resistance that we have embraced for years, destroy it, and try art instead. "Being realistic is nothing more than stalling," he says. "However if you can get the rational part of your brain to listen, pay attention and still facilitate new challenges where you create processes and products that make improvements for many, then you can keep innovation alive."

For cynics, the resistance won a long time ago. They have given up on innovation and continue to convince themselves that they can accomplish nothing better. This cynical self-fulfilling prophecy can become deadweight for other groups in an organization.

There is an important difference between cynics and those who have done the research. When you understand the calculated likelihood of success, those who are intrigued by the challenge will move forward with the project when others will not.

The failure rate for innovation can be high. However, companies need an accepted process that allows for failure and even embraces it. In the book *The Black Swan,* Nassin Talab discussed the impact of the highly improbable and how one must plan for this rarest of events because it may happen. In a statistics class, this would focus on the Poisson Distribution for rare events. If BP had studied this in more depth and planned better for contingencies and backup, far less damage would have occurred during the Gulf Oil Spill.

In manufacturing, processes rarely work the first time. To expect success on the first or even the second attempt sets the company up for disappointment. That's why engineers make prototypes first, test them, see what needs improvement, and make adjustments before mass production begins. To succeed, companies must accept this learning process to create a new product. They must make successive approximations; keep thorough notes and do extensive research.

Edison did this when he improved the light bulb. He knew that if he worked alone it would take a long time to create a working light bulb. However using more scientists who documented what they did achieved success faster.

Edison set his ego aside along with the need to control every test, shared the work with others, made thousands of trials and succeeded. Work is about making a difference in more than just your job, which is about following your duties. Seth Godin says, "If you can get through the resistance and build something that makes a difference, then you have accomplished your work and need to continue with your work." Quit the tasks that distract you from accomplishing your art and do the tasks that take you to the next level.

Action does not equal productivity. Look at the results of people who seem busy. If they act but get no results, they are running in circles. When you act and get results, then you are making progress and your action contributes to accomplishment. When you cope with the problems with class, communication and confidence, you get things done. Look for people who focus their attention on the traits, strengths and virtues that accomplish art and model them in your personal and professional endeavors.

When you select the work you will do, pick a career that is worthy of you. If it is not, pick again and make your work art. Become aware of this process. Ask yourself, "Where did my art go?" E-mail and social media are nice. However e-mail does not change the world. Ask yourself each day what you did for your community, organization or self that will better position you to solve problems for others. This is an art, a process of learning, action, and reflection repeated as a lifestyle.

Anxiety does not protect you. Fears that could come true are rare. However anxiety shows up far too often. It becomes a bad habit that prevents you from realizing your dreams and your goals, the very items that make a difference for everyone else.

You need social intelligence, fear and perception to create your professional art. Continue to learn, practice and improve. Move toward your dream with all your creativity because one size does not fit all. Your gift of making quality art inspires others and changes their lives.

Develop leadership characteristics, including a positive attitude, integrity, trustworthiness, courage, patience, and persistence. Work hard with high energy to build expertise in at least one area.

Research shows that over the years, higher employee engagement results in higher stock prices and higher company value. Why not invest in more effective employee engagement, productivity and systems? Facilitate constructive conversations with people that lead to solutions.

Some people prefer to keep things vague. However, if there is no way to measure progress, how can you have accountability or profits? When someone wants vague, non-process oriented business, be aware that it won't deliver.

There is a difference between dealing with ambiguity and finding a solution. The perception of activity doesn't guarantee productivity, effectiveness or competence. Be careful. If one of your employees acts like a snob while taking care of business rather than with sophistication and professionalism, this might be a result of lack of mastery and inflated ego. It will deliver, at best, hot air!

Specifics or Vagueness...which do you prefer?

Critical thinking can be either logical with process oriented steps or vague with broad brush strokes. Depending on the company, you will get two completely different outcomes and you can guess which one your organization needs. The second method results in the appearance of action, the first method results in hardcore deliverables.

When working with a team, it is also important to consider the key points that make a team successful including enhancing trust, effective communication (including any issues that could pose problems), commitment, accountability and responsibility to follow through with results.

Let's consider what it might be like for an employer in a system where everything is self taught or occasionally guided by a more experienced person.

Consider return on investment first. You are in business to make money. If you can't measure your return on investment, how can you tell if you're making money? Whether this is a for-profit, a non-profit, or government, profit needs to be measured.

Contrary to popular practice, no one has an endless bank account! Business is in business to make a profit and to offer services to customers in the community, country, and world. If you can make money while you sleep, you have leveraged this skill. Whether you are growing fruit on trees or selling electronic products people purchase online, this facilitates your success.

This applies to government as well. China leverages their economy to keep lower level workers content enough to not riot, yet strategically retains a lower price point for goods manufactured in their country. As a result, it is more challenging for others to compete in the global manufacturing market. This draws in income from other countries and builds their economy. If they can maintain their deflated economy for a long period of time, other companies may not weather the competition and may fold. If a country can lower the value of their economy, at what point in their agenda do they raise it?

I came from private industry and worked with government for several years before I returned to the corporate arena. A director at my company discovered that I had a unique background that included HR, Training, Organizational Development and IT. He said, "You are unique in many ways due to your background. Can you send me your resume? I would like to know if you can help us design a program for our clients that are currently being underserved." I sent the information requested and began attending key meetings, addressing gaps in customer delivery and other problems in the organization.

They needed to stop millions of dollars from hemorrhaging out of the company. I asked myself if organizational redesign could improve the infrastructure. We needed to intervene quickly because they had poor knowledge transfer systems in place. Their poor results were a direct result of current workers having inadequate information about how company processes worked. They needed to focus on transferring knowledge and increasing awareness to save money.

During this process a supervisor asked me, "Why are you doing this?" I replied, "It helps people live better lives and saves money." He looked at me with an odd expression. "Why? It's just taxpayer dollars." I said, "You're correct and I'm a taxpayer." He had no answer. I was dumfounded that people could not understand how their actions related to their lives. It felt like a Homer Simpson moment: **"Doh!"** Thank goodness upper management had the vision, wisdom and perspective to understand the short and long term benefits of a systematic redesign and improvement.

In the process of successfully transferring knowledge consider incorporating the following:
Do's
- Develop education and training programs that are in person and blended with E-learning.
- Lead a training program that includes needs assessments, design, development, instruction, facilitation, and program evaluation. The ability to measure this will facilitate understanding the direct return on investment.

- Use adult learning theory, learning styles and adult motivation techniques. (Programs are far more effective when you guide people to leverage their strengths and interests to help meet business goals).
- Determine employee knowledge gaps, then recommend and implement the appropriate training. Be flexible.

Don'ts
- Develop education and training programs that are fragmented and focused on individual experience exclusively (include additional resources to correct for this).
- Don't focus on individual egos since this distracts from the tasks and information needed to learn. It also distracts from the organization's mission and core values.
- Leading elements of a training program – One should NEVER feel like they have reinvent the wheel. It's a waste of money, brains and time.
- Execute projects utilizing limited access to knowledge without considering different learning styles and ignore adult motivation and uniqueness.
- Ignore or don't determine employee skill/knowledge needs because it wastes everyone's time.

7 Steps to Successfully Take the Ouch Out of Your Organization's Financial Pain

How much pain does your organization need to feel financially before it realizes the need for change?

1. Ouch, we need to do something to stop the pain!
2. Idea…Lets diagnose the problem so we can offer the best treatment and get the pain to stop! After all we can't put a band-aid on something that is broken and expect it to work, right?
3. When do we need this to happen? A timeline with milestones.
4. How much longer can we afford to do this? Not much longer. Time is of the essence! This current customer system is a luxury that we can no longer afford. We need to do something better.

5. What are our alternatives and "best practice" options? It takes professional assessment, and strategic planning to effectively address the problem that is causing pain.
6. Take action and fix it!
7. Insure that best practices that protect your organization are in place so this never happens again!

The individual who is best prepared for any occupation is the one…able to adapt himself to any situation. ~Mortimer Smith

References

Cameron, Kim S. (2008). *Positive Leadership: Strategies for Extraordinary Performance*

Collins, Jim (2001). *Good to Great: Why Some Companies Make the Leap and Others Don't*

Godin, Seth (2005). *The Big Moo: Stop Trying to Be Perfect and Start Being Remarkable*

Godin, Seth (2010) *Linchpin: Are You Indispensable?*

Goleman, Daniel (2004). *Primal Leadership: Learning to Lead with Emotional Intelligence*

Pink, Daniel (2009). *Drive: The Surprising Truth About What Motivates Us*

Rock, David (2009). *Your Brain at Work: Strategies for Overcoming Distraction, Regaining Focus, and Working Smarter All Day Long*

Tichy, Noel and Bennis, Warren (2007) *Judgment: How Winning Leaders Make Good Calls*

Zaffron, Steve and Logan, Dave (2009). *The Three Laws of Performance: Rewriting the Future of Your Organization and Your Life*

12

Military Succession Planning Lessons for the Business Community

By Murray Schrantz

In the second century AD, Claudius Galenus discovered that ligature (tying an artery that was bleeding uncontrollably) was a highly effective means of preventing death. As the chief surgeon for wounded gladiators in Pergamum, Turkey, Galen was the first to stop a hemorrhage by tying the injured vessel closed. That discovery reduced the mortality of his patients to next to nothing.

This process would have revolutionized medicine had it not been forgotten for 1,500 years. In 300 BC, the Romans invented concrete (along with the arch, dome, aqueducts), and other structural marvels. Unfortunately, they didn't realize that their success was based on using volcanic ash. Because they didn't know critical details, they unknowingly made huge advances in construction but lacked the ability to convey their knowledge to future generations.[1]

These two examples reflect a continuing, all too familiar problem that faces today's industry and the workforce it employs. The typical approach to succession planning in business, whether in large multinationals or small enterprises, often includes rapid fire decisions based on gut reactions or dredging up archaic HR department policies and procedures that are rarely updated (or even reviewed).

Ultimately executive leadership makes the decisions, which may not reflect previously established policies and procedures. This lack of preparation for planned and unplanned changes in leadership means that key skill sets are often overlooked in the urgency of the moment.

Management can make short to midterm plans to deal with retirements, promotions, and transfers. However, companies must also prepare for unplanned events such as employees finding better jobs elsewhere, sudden and severe medical problems, family emergencies, or even death (witness the effects of the 9/11 attacks on companies such as Sun Microsystems, Oracle, and Cisco).

When these unplanned events happen, the "leaky roof" mentality doesn't work because it causes chaos in management that confuses what should be an otherwise relatively smooth transition.

Management must focus on sound business practices by creating a deliberate process they can implement at all levels of the organization. They must incorporate this paradigm into the organization's mindset so it becomes a recurring ritual of the business enterprise. Avoiding the disruption of sudden choices (and their long term consequences) and the emotional decisions and knee jerk reactions that follow, will result in plans that represent the best interests of the organization.

When an executive level manager leaves, the company typically makes two choices. The first is to identify someone in the organization who is prepared to step in. The alternative is to use an executive search organization to find someone who can fill the position.

The challenge with the former option is that if the candidate is not prepared, further chaos will result. The problem with the latter, even if an appropriate person can be found, is the length of time needed to complete the search, place the person into the organization, and train them appropriately. The ensuing lack of leadership when it is most needed compounds the problems.

The Military Approach

One source of proven ideas to methodically plan a better alternative is our nation's military. Although those unfamiliar with the inner workings of military succession planning may say these methods are antiquated, the services have developed increasingly sophisticated processes to meet crises far more urgent than those encountered in the businesses community.

The military's strategy and doctrine has evolved over the last several hundred years due to changes in threats encountered, technological advances, and our dynamic political environment. It is now a deliberate process that can be painstakingly slow due to entrenched thinking that comes from past successes (while occasionally ignoring failures), an unwillingness to take chances with unproven ideas, and a large organizational structure that can be resistant to change.

As the sole superpower, however, the US military has developed a highly effective model for applying the principles of warfare, as they apply to human resources, that business leaders can learn from. In particular, the succession planning process is a key element that ensures continuity of leadership, stability of operations and achievement of goals in virtually any situation.

Business executives can glean valuable lessons from the military's approach to leadership, particularly as it applies to the organization, training, and development of its leaders. Whether involving a lower level manager or a key executive, good succession planning has a dramatic effect on the function and effectiveness of the organization. To understand the primary opportunities in this approach, we must define the parallels and differences between military structure and that found in business.

First, let's look at the many apparent differences between military practice and civilian business:

- While no direct civilian counterparts to the Uniform Code of Military Justice and the Geneva Conventions exist, civil and criminal laws do limit, to one degree or another, the courses of action available to businesses.
- No lives are routinely lost and no weapons are available to destroy the enemy. However, sudden personnel changes can lead to virtually the same situation and examples exist of businesses that "destroy" their competitors' will to fight, which means they are driven out of business.

- Officers, noncommissioned officers (sergeants), and enlisted personnel are contractually obligated to that service on a 24 hour, 7 day a week basis while on active duty. While this is hardly true in the civilian world, barriers to exiting employment at one company (a weak job market and poor economy, needed health insurance benefits, desirable investment and retirement options, vesting, and the like) can create an effective means of promoting loyalty or at least continuation of service.
- Congressional appropriations for the military are guaranteed, to one degree or the other, and amount to $700 billion in fiscal year 2010[2]. While no commercial enterprise could match that expenditure level on an annual basis, Exxon Mobil had revenues of almost $400 billion in 2007 and a market capitalization of over $450 trillion[3].
- Due to the military's philosophy that their leaders should continue to improve and advance, there is an "up or out" policy for its leaders.[4] That policy, primarily created for commissioned officers and noncommissioned officers, establishes the maximum time allowed for service at certain ranks. In other words, no-one can remain a Captain beyond a certain length of time. A promotions board reviews each service member's performance on two different occasions and either promotes the individual or forces them out. While there may be some considerations of this nature in business, it remains a largely military policy.

This comparison of potential disparities between the two could continue, but this comparison shows that differences between the US military (for the purpose of this proposal) and business enterprises are relatively insignificant.

The Military Model

The military has a formal, well defined configuration of rank in its organizational structure that delineates its leadership and staff positions. It also includes a process for advancement that includes secondary and tertiary roles for individuals to ensure that both commissioned and noncommissioned officers are well prepared for higher levels of responsibility and authority. A formal evaluation system ensures that roles and responsibilities are clearly outlined and that regular evaluations gauge progress against those goals.

The "Efficiency Report System"[5,6], employed for all military personnel, provides a common means to ensure that roles and responsibilities are documented and progress against mutually agreed upon goals is measured. It addresses performance (standards based) and potential. This system requires the "Rater" to evaluate his or her subordinate(s) and includes a similar requirement on a "Senior Rater" that confirms (or comments on) the rating officer's evaluation and also rates the individual against all other individuals of that particular rank. He or she also lists three future jobs/positions that the individual should be considered to fill to broaden the individual in developing leadership abilities. Although this places an additional administrative burden on "Senior Raters" it has advantages:

- Provides an additional perspective for the rated officer's performance
- Avoids, or at least minimizes, personality conflicts between the rater and rated officer, if they exist
- Highlights the progress and reputation of the rated officer (or enlisted person)
- Provides a level of continuity for the rated officer should the "Rater" or "Senior Rater" be new to the position

The military has to operate on a 24/7 basis, which places enormous burdens on leadership. However, it considers the necessity of cross training its leaders to be a vital aspect of preparedness[74]. This requirement states that, in addition to the primary assignment and career track, officers and senior noncommissioned officers (NCOs) must develop proficiency in secondary roles. For example, an infantry officer could have a secondary role in logistics; an artillery officer might have a secondary role as an IT officer. Formal training is required and the officer alternates between assignments in primary and secondary positions.

Adaptation to Business

The challenge to adapting these lessons successfully to business is not a lack of clarity about the need for the processes and procedures involved but rather achieving executive leadership commitment to apply them at all levels of management, particularly senior management. Successful businesses continue to struggle with increased competition and a weaker economic climate while at the same time responding to shareholders' calls for more profits. While downsizing can reap the immediate reward of improving worker productivity and, thereby, profitability in the short run, it places additional demands on the organization's management as it handles added responsibilities with a smaller staff.

Even without reduced manpower, few executives would argue that their organizations, particularly the command structure, have the time and resources available to formalize their performance evaluation system. Most are also not inclined to take leaders from their primary responsibilities and cross-train them in other functional areas. Yet it is precisely those approaches that will serve the long term interests of the organizations.

On December 14, 1993, Rich Snyder, president and son of the founder of the highly successful In-N-Out Burger chain was returning to his headquarters in Southern California on a chartered jet. The company's COO, Philip West, and he had just opened a new store in Fresno and were on final approach to the John Wayne Airport behind a Boeing 757 when their much smaller plane was caught in severe wake turbulence that the large aircraft created. The plane crashed about a mile short of the runway leaving no survivors.

Although Snyder and West had a prior agreement not to fly together, they broke the agreement on that trip. Esther Snyder, who together with her husband had founded the company, had been on the plane but got off at an earlier stop.[8]

(Military policy forbids senior leaders, particularly a commander and his executive officer, from traveling on the same aircraft. While that policy may seem to overreach in a non-combat environment, when accidental deaths such as this one happen, it could mitigate the resulting leadership void.)

How do we adapt these lessons to the contemporary business model?

Develop formal job descriptions for each position within the company.

Meet with each current employee to review those requirements and repeat annually or sooner if there is a major change, e.g. mission requirements, leadership that directly affects that individual.

1. Identify the critical operational and back-office skills needed to keep the company functioning
2. Set up a training program to help employees improve their skills
3. Identify the key personnel that are committed to the business and want to learn more
4. Develop their skills – mentor them
5. Assign responsibility and authority to those who can prove they have learned the skills
6. Think through the "what ifs," the Murphyisms – that are risk management
7. Develop an exit strategy
8. Ensure that good communication is in place and exercise it regularly[9]

As an employee, mirrored personal responsibilities should be pursued. They include:

1. Whether you are a new hire or experienced in your position, ask for a job description (if you don't already have one). If it doesn't exist, write one and submit it to your supervisor for approval. If they have one, review it and recommend needed changes.
2. Create a timeline for completing the responsibilities listed and use this as a basis for a performance review
3. Identify additional skills that would broaden your value to the company (to fill other positions that appeal to you and likewise benefit the organization) and identify the training necessary to acquire those skills (to include needed training for primary responsibilities if any holes exist).
4. Ask for additional authority and responsibility to perform supplementary tasks and/or job classifications.

The importance of identifying, developing, and training subordinates is an essential part of succession planning and helps ensure the successful continuity of the business enterprise. The military's approach to providing the appropriate depth of leadership in key areas can serve as a model for industry. In 1991, Jack Welch said, "From now on, choosing my successor is the most important decision I'll make. It occupies a considerable amount of thought almost every day."[10] That's a pretty strong statement for someone who had the vision and leadership ability to increase the value of General Electric from $13 billion to $410 billion dollars during his tenure.

In 1995, GE's transportation business, struggling to attract top notch talent at its headquarters in Erie, PA, began recruiting junior military officers. So successful were they that other GE units did the same. When GE had 80, Jack Welch, GE's CEO, asked all of them to come to the Fairfield, CT offices where he spent an entire day with them. Impressed with the quality and track record of the recruits, he insisted that the company hire 200 junior military officers annually. In less than three years, GE had 711 of them on the payroll and many have already gained significant promotions.[11] Perhaps recruiting military officers into business positions isn't always needed or even appropriate. For Jack Welch, however, it paid off.

The military has not always been a flawless source of the processes described. There have been notable failures of leadership in developing subordinates. A rather dismal example is the case of Navy Captain Holly Graf, the first woman to command both a destroyer and, later, a cruiser. She was on a fast track to rise to the highest ranks in the Navy, but her berating, demeaning leadership style became her undoing. More than a few officers under her command left the service as a direct result of their experiences on her ships.[12] While there is little to excuse that performance (or lack thereof) despite repeated official complaints, the question that begs to be asked is "where were her superiors during this troubling time?" Had she been abandoned to self-destruct without the supervision and concern that should be especially strong for a woman with such potential who had been placed in such critical and visible positions? This demonstrates the need to not only have a well developed succession plan but to implement and nurture it to ensure success.

Once again, the ability to adapt to changing threats in a dynamic marketplace is a hallmark of successful businesses and individuals. Those same traits of leadership, foresight, and imagination that create a competitive edge today, can serve as a platform for future.

[1] *Cracked* magazine article by David Graham, April 26, 2010

[2] *Updated Summary Tables* Budget of the U.S. Government, dated May 2009 Table S-6, page 13

[3] ExxonMobil 2008 *Financial and Operating Review*, page 2

[4] Military.com February 6, 2009

[5] AR 623-105 dated 1 April 1998

[6] DA Form 67-9

[7] Army Pamphlet 600-3

[8] "Top In-N-Out Burger Execs Killed in Calif. Plane Crash", *Nation's Restaurant News,* January 3, 1994, pp. 1-2

[9] "Life's Lessons in Business" Tom Niewulis Blog dated 12/2/09

[10] http://www.ameinfo.com/59276.html May 4, 2005

[11] "How Jack Welch Runs GE" *Business Week*, June 8, 1998

[12] *Time* magazine, Mark Thompson, March 3, 2010

13

Hiring an Executive Recruiter

By Mark Fierle

This discussion will be from the company point of view. After all it is the company that hired me to find the candidate they desired. With this in mind, over the course of many years I counseled some of the finest organizations (big and small) in America. I often found that the decision maker I was working with had a great deal of experience in their field of expertise but very little in the "art of interviewing." In fact they only interviewed candidates once or twice per year. Because interviewing took them away from what they were being paid to do, it was a pain to do and it was done in a less than stellar and informed manner. It often led to uneven results, some good, some ok, and many not good at all!

Reasons not to use a Search Firm

Two questions often come up when I speak to executives about using a search firm. Why should they use a search firm and why should they pay a fee? I don't know which question comes first although I greatly expect it's often fees.

Generally these questions come from executives that have never used a search firm or have had a bad experience in the past. I often get the impression that using a search firm can be almost as painful as buying a used car from Slick, the used car salesman.

Here are some guidelines that will help.

Do not use a search firm if, repeat **do not** use if:

- You are **not** having problems identifying and hiring the best possible candidates (not just the best you are seeing) through your normal sources.
- It is **not** important to have this position staffed on a timely basis.
- The real costs, advertising, evaluating resumes, categorizing, prioritizing, verifying credentials, being without a person in that position, having offers rejected, having the candidate quit after a short time on the job, executive time, etc. are all **NOT** a factor.
- It is your impression that there are a lot of great candidates in the job market that are just drooling to come to work for you. Editorial comment: there are only so many truly superior candidates available (in good times and bad) and they are generally sought after and don't use internet search engines.
- Your expectations are unrealistic, unattainable, or a real stretch. Again, an executive recruiter is generally engaged to find qualified candidates, not needles in a haystack.

These are a few reasons not to use a search firm. However, if identifying great candidates, saving time, and expectations are factors, it might be time to consider using a search firm.

Here are some thoughts that may be helpful in choosing one.

What type should you use, contingency or retained? If time is important and you want to see a select number of qualified candidates and are ready to choose the best of those seen, choose a contingency firm. If time is not an urgent factor, or you need extensive recruiting to develop a candidate pool, use a retained firm.

A current trend is to hire a firm that uses a **partnership** agreement. This is a combination of the contingency/retained agreement and works like a partnership. It is designed to share the risk. Instead of paying all up front as in retained, a percentage is paid up front to cover part of the recruiter's expenses. Better yet, if you have confidence in a particular recruiter, discuss which format is more appropriate with them. The result is the same, and that's what counts.

If you are doing a contingency search, choose **only one recruiter**. Settle on a reasonable time during which you wish to see the pool of candidates they recruit and evaluate for you, then use just him/her.

Good suggestion: Don't get caught up in the notion that you will see better candidates if you use a combination of your own resources and multiple search firms. If a recruiter knows you are using them exclusively they will generally do extra work to get what you want. Consider this: You cannot expect a recruiter to work for free. That's what you are setting them up for when you use multiple sources. Nobody wants to expend all their resources on you if there is a chance they will not be paid for it. Use one and they will do the best possible job for you.

Selecting a Firm

This is an art, but not unlike going to a bank for a loan. Here are some thoughts:

- Get to know the recruiter before you need them. Accept their calls, get to know them and in turn they get to know you and your company. Good chemistry is a plus.
- Ask them how they work, how the process works, and what they need from you. This is necessary for them to deliver for you.
- Ask them for literature on their firm. Ask whether they are accredited, do they belong to trade-groups, how long have they been in business? Ask how their agreement works. Be wary of firms that put a stamp on a resume and expect you to pay a fee based on that!
- Ask what they expect of you.
- Insist on qualified candidates only.

As a final thought, the best recruiters are a resource to you. High performance staff candidates are not normally looking for another position. Sometimes they are like a thoroughbred horse and require special handling. While they may not be actively looking, most of them keep their ears open to good opportunities. These are the type of candidates that you will find best through a search firm. The key criterion is qualified. A good search consultant, with your cooperation, will deliver.

Now let's look at the search itself.

A User's Guide

In today's marketplace, organizations often think that there is a wealth of talent available for the asking. This expectation level often comes from above and leads to unsuccessful searches where truly superior candidates can be missed. Here are some ways to ensure the search assignment is successful.

To avoid most problems, focus on several key areas:

- **Set clear ground rules.** Questions to ask include: What are the dynamics of the search assignment, the goals, expectations, timing, sources, how many candidates do we want to evaluate, and who in the company is in charge of the search? These are good starting points.
- **How difficult is the assignment?** When working with a search firm, questions include access to enough target companies to recruit candidates, background and experience requirements, which are desirable, and where compromises can be made.
- **Compensation.** A good search firm will generally present you with candidates that you would have a difficult time finding on your own. Often clients are stalled at the level of compensation that the best people command. It is important that the search consultant give you a clear idea of what it will take to get the best candidates. This will ease disappointment.
- **How will the interview be conducted?** The search consultant should have a clear idea of the types of questions that will be asked, length of the interview, and who the candidate will see. The goal is to have both a prepared interviewer and candidate. This will help in getting the truly superior candidates and not just the best interviewers.
- **Deciding on the best candidates.** Failure in a search is often the result of decision makers postponing making a decision. Superior candidates will often not be available if the decision is postponed beyond a reasonable time. After all, would you want to work for a company that can't make a decision? A

good idea is to be up front with how the decision making process will go. A good search consultant, when informed, can be a resource for keeping the candidate "on ice" if necessary.

- **The offer.** In the American enterprise system the company wants to pay the least and the candidate wants to get the most. Negotiations can be embarrassing to both. This is where the best search consultants earn their fee by making an offer that will be accepted.
- **A Business partnership.** Successful partnerships have good communication networks. The company should expect candidates that are qualified, presented in a timely manner, and who promptly answers when questions are asked.

The search consultant expects the company to see the candidates, give feedback in a timely manner, and agree upon "where do we go from here" questions. When a search is not meeting expectation levels, it's good to review the ground rules. It may be time to re-establish expectations.

Now the actual interview: *"Keys to Effective Interviewing"*

Experience

Effective interviewing is an ever changing process. However, there are still some never-changing techniques that can both improve your interviewing skills and help you hire the best candidates.

Making the Most of Your Time

Interviewing is a disruption of your normal daily routine. It can be even more disruptive when you are trying to fill a key position. Seeing four or five people over a period of weeks can be highly unproductive because you forget key information about the first applicants by the time you see the final applicant. Even more important, the prime candidate can have lost interest or taken another position before you complete the decision making process.

Finding a Good Match

If we could limit interviewing to only objective issues we would have a more exact science. However, since we generally cannot, how do we increase the odds of finding a good match?

Here are some easy rules. It is best to approach the interview without pre-conceived ideas of what the best candidate will look like. This will often inhibit the search. For example, there is no magic in certain degrees or years of experience. However, often interviewers get themselves "hung up" on these criteria. What is important? The answer is simple: focus on the job duties and who can do them!

Here are some simple steps to follow:

1. Make a list of job duties.
2. Decide which duties have the highest priority.
3. Direct your questions to uncover those candidates that can perform these duties most effectively.

Conducting the Interview

The interview process should achieve three key objectives:

1. Expose experience that qualifies the candidate for your job.
2. Will the candidate's personality fit your company culture?
3. Sell the candidate on the opportunity.

To ensure the best basis of comparison, it is important to ask the same set of questions of each candidate. Some refer to this as a "Model Interview." Prepare the model interview before you meet the first candidate. First develop a series of questions to include professional experience, technical knowledge, and career accomplishments relevant to each person. Have this model typed, leaving room for answers, and duplicate the form for use with each candidate. For your help I have included a sample model interview for your review.

Staging the Interview

Best way to get into the interview is to focus on the purpose of the meeting and keep small talk to a minimum. Introduce yourself by name and title. "We are interviewing for a Manager of MIS, so let's talk about your experience."

What Will Key Questions Reveal

Using your model interview sheet as a guide, get the basic information you want from each candidate. Don't hesitate to ask each to clarify, expand upon, or elaborate when you want to demonstrate initiative, motivation, attitude, management, or organizational skills.

Be sure to ask open ended questions that can't be answered yes or no. Here are some examples:

Initiative: What career accomplishments are you most proud of? What did you dislike most about your most recent position? What did you do to change it?

Motivation: What are your goals for the next two years? Five years? What have you done to achieve your goals?

Attitude: How competitive are you? Please elaborate. How do you feel about routine work?

Management and Organizational Skills: Describe how you spend a typical day. What is your management style? How do you handle marginal employees?

When You Talk About Money

You don't talk about the size of the diamond on the first date. Therefore, don't talk about compensation on the first interview. Once you have determined that you have found someone who can do the job, it's time to talk about compensation. This gives you an opportunity to sell the candidate on the company and the opportunity.

Selling the Opportunity

When you complete the basic interview process and you like what you have heard, don't assume the candidate is eager to go to work for you. Make sure the candidate leaves your interview with enthusiasm. Do this whether or not you intend to make an offer or pass the candidate on to others for additional interviews.

Your ability to highlight the benefits of working with your company can make the difference. Here are some points to emphasize:

Industry: Stability, growth, and cyclical fluctuations are areas to discuss.

Company: How does your company compare? What makes your company stand out from your competitors?

Position: Why is the position available? Where does it lead? What will the candidate gain in career growth? How much visibility will there be in the corporation?

Environment: What is the culture of the company, your management style, and physical amenities?

Put this together, summarize your thoughts on candidates, and prepare a chart to record your reactions. On the left side: reasons to hire. On the right side: areas of concern. You will be surprised how easy the decision making process will be.

Selection Time

With the market seemingly full of candidates, a company will often put off the selection process hoping to find the one perfect candidate. There is no such thing! That's why it is important to focus on the job duties and who can do them. Often the candidate you like best does not come in first; that's why you must establish the real **needs** and get the most out of the interviewing process.

A Final Thought

When you find the best candidate, consider that they might have another option. Cut the red tape to accelerate the process. Unnecessary delays often send the wrong signals and the candidate becomes disenchanted or loses interest. When this occurs, you end up going back to square one.

Sample Model Interview

On your actual **Model Interview** sheet leave space after each question for candidate response.

Professional Experience and Technical Knowledge

- Describe your last three years of work experience. What were your responsibilities?
- The three most important duties we want you to perform are:

   A. _____

   B. _____

   C. _____

   What experience do you have that would qualify you to perform these tasks?
- What background experience do you have that would be beneficial to our company?

Career Accomplishments and Creativity
- What career accomplishments are you most proud of?
- How can these accomplishments be transformed to our company's benefit?
- What suggestions did you make at your last job to improve your company's operations?

Motivation & Attitude
- What personal goals did you set at your last job?
- How well did you accomplish them?
- How do you feel about routine assignments?

Character & Personality
- What are your outside interests?
- What are your strengths? Weaknesses?
- How would you describe your personality?

Using these techniques will help you find the key person or people that you are looking for.

Again it is an art, not a science, but the better the strategy and tactics you use the better results you can expect.

Finally I suggest you read the chapters in this book of interest several times or more. You will find that ideas become apparent that may have been overlooked previously and this can change your outlook. I once had a candidate that I had recruited for an important position. He worked for a famous international maker of binoculars. After we finished all the prep work, he sent me a pair of binoculars with a note saying, "Thanks for keeping your eyes open for me." What a surprise gift that was! The moral is keep your eyes open and be prepared.

110 Adapt or Perish

Section 2

Adapting Leadership

Improving Your Performance

112 Adapt or Perish

14

Becoming the Risk Averse Organization

By Ilene Albert-Nelson

Protecting What You Have Instead of Embracing Change

Has your company started protecting what it has instead of looking for the next great opportunity?

Many companies seem to hit a tipping point where they go from entrepreneurial organizations that drive growth, embrace change and actively seek new markets to being very risk averse, change averse ("this is the way we do it here") and just want play where they are comfortable.

With this, organizations often go from hiring "hunters" to only hiring "farmers", which reinforces this change.

And it seems the larger the organization, the more likely this is to happen. It also seems to happen when companies merge – the "farmer" organization often seems to win out in the end.

Why does this happen? Human nature! People like the comfortable, they like the predictable and they like routine. An organization that embraces change and looks to reinvent itself constantly runs right up against these needs that most people have. Face it, most people are risk averse and don't like change at all.

What is the result of this? A company that stops growing because it starts fighting for more of the pie that it already has and becomes more inward focused than focused on new places to grow. At some point, they reach the point of diminishing returns for growth (market share) or the pie starts shrinking (technology changes). A company that becomes risk averse becomes obsolete. What happened to all the buggy whip companies that never started making anything else when the automobile took over from horses? Is this your company?

So how do you keep your company from becoming risk averse?
A few ideas:

- **Don't let the system become the driving force** – are you working for the system or is the system working for you? Bureaucracy may be helpful but too much kills any entrepreneurial spirit in the organization.
- **Make sure you hire diverse personality types.** Risk averse organizations hire people that act like they do, have the same personality profiles they do and have the same types of work histories. They don't want to be challenged and they don't want to manage conflict.
- **Keep divisions as small as you can** so people know each other and can do things without large meetings, layers and lots of approvals. Too many hands in the pie lead to mediocrity. Those jokes about products created by committees are true.
- **Celebrate and encourage risk** – it takes some failures to find successes. Risk averse companies don't want to see any failure and punish all failure instead of understanding that some failure may ultimately help learning and lead to big wins. If failure happens, look for the why not the who. Then internalize the lessons, learn and move on.
- **Think outside the box you are in today.** Just because your sales force doesn't call on that channel or just because you don't have that skill set internally doesn't mean that you can't hire it, learn it or figure it out.
- **Don't committee new ideas to death.** Committees have a tendency to merge to the middle and to the least risky solution that protects everyone's status quo.

- **The role of management is to remove obstacles,** provide counsel and cheerlead the team that is running with the idea. Unless what they want to do is so risky that it could bring down the organization or damage the company's reputation, management shouldn't be the ones calling the shots. Let the team closest to the research and the idea execute. This goes back to allowing failure; one of the best things someone said to me when I was trying to start a new brand was, "I reserve the right to say 'I told you so,' but you are the ones closest to the consumer and have the passion for what you are doing so go do it."
- **Don't bring in outside consultants to help unless asked.** Outside consultants will often tell management what they want to hear (who is paying their bill anyway?) and may not understand the market or the opportunity as well as the internal team. It is a real de-motivator to the team to have management so clearly communicate that they don't trust or believe what the team is telling them!
- **Have a line in the budget to support new ideas** that come up during the year so they can be explored without major presentations or restructuring of existing budgets. Want to really kill new ideas? Take budget from existing businesses that are already approved. This puts the idea team at odds with the existing businesses and increases the likelihood that the organization will neither support nor assist the team with the new idea.
- **Make sure the organization knows** that they can pursue new ideas that create new growth. If your team is afraid to go in new directions or suggest new businesses, then you are already in a risk-averse organization.
- **Beware of the sheep in wolf's clothing.** Many companies say they want to embrace change and entrepreneurial spirit but they really don't. The organization stifles the entrepreneurs and forces them out because they are different or too assertive. What large company doesn't talk about wanting to be entrepreneurial and say they embrace change? That isn't really who they are for the most part. The corporate structure is heavily invested in the status quo. That structure has been built

and staffed to support that business model. There are some examples of large companies who are game changers (Apple being the most public example) but this is rare.

Has your company become risk averse? Are you spending more time filling out paperwork and serving on committees that serve the current business model and the current businesses? Who is thinking about the game changer? Anyone? If not, maybe it should be you.

15

Being a Risk Taker

By Steve Amos

Will America Keep Taking Risks? Everyone has seen the news about Japan's Fukushima Daiichi nuclear leaks. These second generation 1970's nuclear plants survived a very rare 9.0 earthquake and properly shut down. What did not survive was the generators when hit with tsunami twice the size they were suppose to survive.

Before that we had the Deep Horizon oil platform exploding, burning and sinking in the Gulf of Mexico. This large oil spill is memorable, as are the news stories reporting on the people who are negatively affected. Very heart wrenching.

The press is ripping British Petroleum as incompetent evil money makers. BP has responded with an announcement that they are doing everything they can to clean up the problem, and will pay for all the damages. Properly so, I may add.

The real question is what will happen long term. Will either of these be like the Three Mile Island accident, where the nuclear industry fell behind the rest of world in developing nuclear energy? Think about it. One accident caused a whole industry to stop in its tracks over 30 years ago. Almost no new plants have been built for three decades.

118 Adapt or Perish

What is the result? Most nuclear technology has moved to other countries. Canada and France have developed much stronger nuclear electricity technology.

The other scary side effect of risk reluctance is that modern plants were supposed to replace the older plants after 25 to 30 years. Instead 30, 40 and 50-year-old plants are patched up and kept running because the utilities cannot replace them with modern, more efficient and safer plants. The political risk is so high that the financial cost becomes prohibitive. Who knows that the newer third generation plants survived the same earthquake and tsunami safely next to the failed plants?

Will one oil spill stop more drilling and exploration? Will the US be more dependent on oil imports to provide the gasoline and diesel our cars and trucks need or the fertilizer our farmers need? Most of us drive cars and all of us buy groceries and goods delivered by truck. Are we going to stop producing the energy we need to compete in a global economy?

Over 30,000 drilling platforms dot the Gulf of Mexico, providing plenty of opportunities for more accidents and oil spills. Will we stop driving and eating? No. We cannot stop taking reasonable risks.

We do not live in a risk free world. There is no way to prevent every danger and make everyone safe. What will happen if we don't take reasonable risks?

Often we learn more from failure than from success. I am concerned with the "everyone wins" approach to raising children. If everyone gets a prize, what is the reward for hard work and sacrifice? What happens when someone who has never failed does fail?

Businesses learn from failure. Google originally wanted to develop a better search engine and then sell it to someone else. That didn't work. Their next idea was to take donations to cover expenses. That wouldn't work as a business. The third business model was to provide a better search engine and sell advertising targeted to the user, which became the successful business we know today.

Our military is trained to take risks. They deliberately get in harms way and fight enemies who want to kill them. We don't see them hiding in a military base in the US. We see our men and women all over the world in the worst conditions performing admirably. They prepare for the risks and use training to overcome them.

When military units are defeated, our military analyzes what went wrong. Why did the field leader make the decisions they did in that situation? What should have been the correct strategy? What tactics, techniques and communication are necessary in the field? What lessons did we learn? How can we train our leaders to do better next time? Leaders and instructors have to study everything and then implement the lessons learned. This is why our military has performed so well for so many years. They take responsibility for their warriors and always look for ways to improve.

Militaries are trained in how to deal with failure. Retreats are failures done in an organized way to minimize losses. They know it is better to fail now rather than waste people, resources and money on a failed strategy. In addition, look at the military cemeteries around the world. We honor those who lost their life defending our countries and don't hide from losing someone in service.

The US has to keep drilling for oil and build nuclear plants as well as developing alternatives, which will take decades to resolve. In the meantime talented men and women will come up with solutions to these problems and improve processes to make them safer. We must continue to develop energy and take risks to succeed.

Your business has to take risks to succeed. You have to develop new products and services. You have to introduce products into the market and see if they succeed or fail.

Ask yourself: Who is the product for? What s the total market? What will this do? What behavior will this product or service change?

Google is a good example of a company that tries new services and products. Look at all the services and options they have developed and introduced. Look at the tabs on the top of the screen. Click more and see what is offered. Did all of these options make money? No. But the successful products and services have increased Google's dominance of their niche selling targeted advertising. It has become a verb to Google something or someone. That is a successful market position.

I started this article with a question: Will America keep taking risks? The question now is: Will your business keep taking risks? Will you celebrate the failures as well as the successes with your team? Will you lead your business to take necessary risks to succeed?

120 Adapt or Perish

$$16$$

Personal and Professional Development Applied

by VaNessa Vollmer, Psy.D

Individual professional and personal development is a lifetime process. I learned this through a series of experiences at different points in my working life.

When I worked in Human Resources at a large organization, I submitted a cost reduction idea that would save the organization over $1,000,000 per year in annual operating expenses. My boss at the time thanked me for the idea and told me that they would implement it.

He added that he wanted to promote me into management but couldn't because I had only an Associate degree, not the required Bachelors Degree. This surprised me since I thought the company would promote me on the merits of my contributions to the bottom line.

He told me, "You need to get a Bachelors degree. It can be in anything, like underwater basket weaving, because it shows two things: first, you can set a goal and second, you can take the necessary steps to achieve that goal. These are the same behaviors we need in management."

I'd worked at this company for several years in professional development, job bidding, and educational reimbursement. Over the years, several people took my advice, returned to school to get more education, and moved up the corporate ladder. The irony is that it was now my turn to take my own advice and return to school to make myself more valuable in business.

I had started work on a Certificate in Human Resources Management but, after my discussion with my boss, it was clear that a Bachelors Degree was mandatory in the professional community.

I asked my boss what he majored in at college and he answered Psychology. I asked him to write me a letter of recommendation so I could return to school. Along with that letter, I took his pearls of wisdom and returned to UC Irvine to complete my Bachelors Degree.

While working on my degree, I decided to go straight through to graduate school to give me even more value and ensure that lack of education became a non-issue in the future. I completed my Masters and Doctorate degrees.

Adult learning theory taught me to apply what I learned as soon as I studied a concept to make the lesson more likely to stick.

For example, I learned in Sociology of Aging that if you don't take advantage of opportunities to enjoy life now, you may regret not doing so when you're older. However, if you have wonderful experiences and create great memories when you're young, later when you're older you will look back over a life filled with abundance, happiness, joy, and a sense of accomplishment.

As a result of these insights, I committed myself to the pursuit of high quality experiences and happiness with my family and friends. One way I "made happy moments" was through entertaining, where I used creative ideas to make enjoyable memories for those in my life. Great food, great friends and great times emerged from dinner get-togethers with fun themes and great homemade food. This kicked up the happiness factor in my life and the life of others.

I implemented these working hypotheses to see if they worked. They have so far.

At graduate school, my intensive studies left little time for fun. Only a few days separated the old and the new quarters. If I didn't plan ahead for my fun time, it wouldn't happen and the weekend would be consumed with chores and errands then be gone in an instant. Determined to have fun before I returned to the books, I would make plans to go to amusement parks, ride roller coasters, or hike into the woods and have an outdoor barbecue dinner with friends as a way to enjoy life and create happy memories at low cost.

I provided an enriched result for everyone. During the holidays, I'd make stuffed Cornish game hens for each person. I'd get them for a good price, serve them with fresh veggies and a creative dessert, and develop an adventure for the taste buds. People grinned as stories, jokes and laughter filled the evening air. Great memories were created to enrich the moment and for everyone to reflect on over the years.

When I was young, I heard a great musical commercial, "Do you remember the times of your life…" When I was very young, commercials told us to "Save those Kodak moments." In fact if you went to Disneyland, signs throughout the park would say, "This is a Kodak photo spot." From exposure to these ideas early in my busy life, I realized that I needed to create those special moments to save and remember. I heard comments from others. "If you do what you love, then you will never work another day in your life." Like a sponge, I soaked up knowledge and walked this talk. I continued to learn new things and apply them to everyday life.

What are the takeaways? To create a healthy balance in life I set my priorities so I could address **impulses vs. plans**, **order my priorities from most important to least important**; and **manage my time**.

As an example of how to use this process, let's say you decide to read *War and Peace* by Leo Tolstoy. A day or a few hours is not enough to accomplish this goal. However, if you schedule time over several weeks, you are more likely to accomplish it, one page at a time.

Let's say a friend calls and asks, "Would you like to go to the movies Saturday night?" You'd say, "Let me check my calendar. Oh, it looks like I have plans. Thanks for asking."

This way you honor your schedule, goals and relationships. It is not necessary to tell your friend what you have planned, just that you have plans. This way you maintain your friendship and honor your goal of reading *War and Peace*. This also applies to completing your education, getting a certificate or taking a class in a subject of personal or professional interest.

On the other hand, if you want spontaneous friendships keep yourself open to sharing quality time with a friend and reschedule your reading into another time slot. This nurtures your relationships and keeps your personal goals on track while keeping a healthy balance between work and play.

When you set goals and schedule every moment so tightly that there's no room for spontaneity or friends, it could affect your health, the health of your relationships, and the quality of your life. In some cases when you are so busy, friends understand this temporary situation and remain in silent support while you finish.

On the other hand, you may know people who are so driven that they carry a stopwatch and believe there is no margin for human error. How does this affect the quality of their relationships, fun and life?

Success is a process leading to lessons and achievement. Like a road trip, you have a destination and a process that gets you there and safely returns you home.

However, there are ways to enrich your travels by enjoying the views and points of interest along the way.

I researched ahead of time for one road trip with some friends. Along the way, we discovered one of the roads to our destination was unexpectedly closed. For some this was bad news as they didn't really want to drive the extra six hours to make it to the hotel we had reserved. Others were elated that they would see more new vistas along the scenic route. Who do you suppose enjoyed the trip more?

 One of the people who enjoyed the extra scenery mentioned that someone they know carries a stop watch on their trips and would have thought this necessary detour was a complete disaster. They noticed that staying flexible and focused on getting to our destination made the trip much more enjoyable and fun for everyone.

These valuable learning opportunities can improve the way we deal with challenges that face us at work and in life. Would you prefer to work with or have a relationship with someone who stays focused on the goal or someone who stresses out and has a bad attitude if things don't go a certain way?

In this case, we respected each other, worked together as a team, and enjoyed the rest of the trip with great food; panoramic views, shared stories, told jokes and laughter filled the air. By the end of the trip they remarked that this was one of the best trips in a long time and reminded them of the fun enjoyed in their childhood.

Everyone has different styles. Some people meet unexpected challenges better than others. Answer these questions to see where you stand.

- What is different about those you know who panic or threaten others out of fear and loss of control?
- What is different about those who get the tools and skills needed to accomplish successful results?
- What are your styles and strengths? How would you like to be different? Who do you know that is like who you want to be? Talk with them, ask questions and learn.

Adaptation and Healthy Development

A genuinely healthy person can balance achieving goals with being spontaneous while nurturing relationships. Learn skills to cope when changes in priorities cause stress. You feel more in control in your life. Many things in life are unexpected. How we deal with them makes a difference for ourselves and others in our life. Understanding different perspectives, listing priorities and aligning your actions improves your health, work relationships, and quality of life.

Some people adapt easier while more rigid people have a harder time dealing with change. Remember nature's model: the brittle tree that can't bend, breaks in the wind while the flexible willow survives the storm. People, like trees, need to find a strong structure that works for the long term but remains flexible enough to maintain healthy relationships.

On the other hand, it is not healthy to have no stress in your life. Even positive events like graduations, new jobs, weddings, and having children cause good stress. When negative events that cause bad stress like poor health, accidents, divorce, job loss, and financial changes occur, protecting the quality of our lives depends on how we adapt.

Choices as Ongoing Adaptations

The Greeks said the only constant is change. We must deal with change effectively to gain success, achieve our professional goals, and nurture our personal friendships. We must also deal with change when we choose not to work in a traditional organization and instead become an entrepreneur where we must build and sustain business relationships. Other great sources include Tony Robbins, Zig Ziglar,

John Maxwell, and Jim Rohn, who all wrote extensively to help people grow personally and build a better image of themselves. Personal and professional growth other than formal school leading to a degree is necessary for a balanced, holistic approach to change, mediating risk, and professional development.

Opting to enjoy success in both our personal and professional lives is a healthy choice. When you are in transition, use this valuable time to reflect, take a step back, and reassess what you liked and what you didn't like in your last work experience.

You can opt for the entrepreneur path and hire yourself or you can continue looking for a job with a great organization. For many, the shift to entrepreneurship is a good way to adapt during challenging economic times because sole proprietorships and small businesses address new needs and create many new opportunities.

Organizational Paradigms

What is Corporate Culture?

Wikipedia defines organizational culture as "an idea in the field of organizational studies and management which describes the psychology, attitudes, experiences, beliefs and values (personal and cultural) of an organization. It has been defined as the specific collection of values and norms that people and groups in an organization share and that control the way they interact with each other and with stakeholders outside the organization." (Wikipedia, 2010)

How does this paradigm shift work in organizations? It creates corporate culture, branding the organization as holding values and beliefs and behaving in a way that aligns it with those beliefs and nuances to make it unique.

Why is this important? This shift applies to organizations no matter their size or geographic region (local, national, or international) or the way they do business. For instance, some organizations can attract employees but can't retain them. These organizations eventually get a reputation as a company that churns and burns because they go through employees so fast. The company puts little investment into the employee because management sees them as a short-term investment.

The "sink or swim" or "trial by fire" methods of bringing new employees into the organization requires minimal effort.

The alternatives require organizations to assist employees through the onboarding process, including corporate integration to facilitate professional development, mentorship, and genuine transformation for short and long term success. Any type of organization, for profit, non-profit, or public service can do this.

Employees watch for these differences and know that if they hire on to a "sink or swim" company, they may get chewed up, burnt out, and expelled quickly. Most people who experience this will share their story with other professionals, giving the organization a "churn and burn" reputation that makes them NOT the employer of choice, but an organization to avoid, except for the desperate or egomaniacs. When there are few jobs, these organizations have an abundance of talent to hire and chew through them without regard for consequences. However, in times of economic growth, they will find informed talent scarcer and will continue to prey on unsuspecting people who walk through their doors.

That's why you need to know if the issue affects just one situation or if it's a trend. If it's a trend, you need to determine if it is short or long term so you can make informed decisions and go in aware of what the company is like. Some call this planning for the worst and hoping for the best, while others call it wishful thinking.

As a prospective employee or new hire assessing an organization, it is wise to have options and Plan B in place in case this high risk situation turns into a high risk outcome.

Best Fit, Aligned Values and Stress Adaptations

Human factors psychology, which works with the effects of the work environment on the individual, backs this up. This approach comes from general systems theory and emphasizes getting the best fit between person and organization. This best culture fit includes ethics, alignment of professional values, and how they deal with or tolerate stressful situations.

When dealing with physical stress like working out at the gym, your body creates a chemical reaction. Lactic acid builds up and if you don't do anything about it, you get fatigued, tight, and have sore muscles.

However, when you get a massage and someone else moves your muscles, you get a different type of chemical reaction where lactic acid is removed from the muscles and water allows you to get rid of the excess buildup and return to better health. The right balance between stress and performance needs can be optimized through improved communication with the brain's chemistry rather than against a stressful reaction.

Just as stress affects the body, stress affects the muscles of the organization, its employees. For example, the Yerkes-Dodson law says that people work best at a moderate level of arousal. When a person becomes fatigued, he or she will perform more poorly in both simple and complex tasks. This increased stress affects job performance and eventually the health of your employees.

Jobs in which the individual has very little control over tasks or work environment often lead to employees experiencing stress disorders. People adapt by taking physical or psychological control over their work environment.

It is common knowledge among air conditioning professionals that some industrial and business offices have thermostats that aren't attached to any wiring. These placebo thermostats provide stress control for some employees without throwing off the climate stability in the rest of the building. Even if the temperature change doesn't work immediately, the employees will likely attribute it to the system taking longer to adjust than they'd like. In the meantime they return to work and wait to see what happens.

Likewise, during this stressful paradigm shift for local business, with several organizations going through national and international mergers and acquisitions, it is even more important to understand how the culture of an organization operates and promotes through shared values and beliefs. When the organizational culture is strong, the group tends to be more cohesive and performance is higher. However, when the culture is less cohesive productivity tends to be lower and distractions higher. National cultures and belief systems also influence organizational culture. Each cultural belief system comes with strengths and areas to improve. Consider looking at key areas to understand how it operates, communicates and implements projects through processes.

In years past, according to Hofstede, the five areas of corporate culture included:

- power distance (meaning small or large variations in power distribution or equal distribution)
- uncertainty avoidance or tolerance of ambiguity
- individualism
- energy with an emphasis on quantity versus quality of life
- long term, future focus versus present situations

While many people have reviewed his work and have tended to oversimplify cultures to identify them with nations, a more timeless aspect of culture over time is its resistance to change in spite of instability.

Effectiveness in the global economy requires further adaptation to differentiate between who won't make it, who will merely survive, and who will take it to the next level, innovate and thrive.

It's critical for organizations to adapt with effective communication systems that work best in your market.

If you have organizations that go into rapid growth mode in the High Tech Industry but do not have the high tech infrastructure to support doing business, which includes training, coaching, and empowering its employees to succeed within the organization, how will this affect your employees and business? It will be distracting, slow processes down, and decrease productivity.

Always create a business mission and congruent values consistent with an adequate infrastructure to support daily work flow. If this minimal investment is not made in advance, employees will become distracted and put their energy elsewhere.

For instance, instead of working on improving their product, supporting their team or providing customer service, they may wonder why the information bandwidth is insufficient to support their projects.

Where does their focus go?

Are they doing their job?	Taking Responsibility
Solving an infrastructure problem?	Distracted & Redeployed
Derailed by frustration?	Avoid/Ignore
Shame and Blaming situation or others?	Rationalization

Employees react to this gap in several ways. Some will do the best they can in a limited environment. Others want to help remove the gap so the company can do business more effectively. Others will draw back, get frustrated and have no idea what to do to make their job function or project better. Still others will tell management about the problem. Others may shame and blame the problems on others. The last category will just leave the organization. Which type of employee do you want to hire for your organization?

Does your organization support employees taking responsibility?

The current system will produce more of the same unless the organization changes the processes, procedures and beliefs fostered in the organization. Is there a clear picture of what success looks like for them? Do the policies and procedures support alignment with talent development?

In one organization the message encouraged employees to return to school for more formal education to meet the business requirements of customers. Many technicians took advantage of company sponsorship to earn a degree. However, when the degree was achieved and acknowledged, the company did not raise the individual's income to equal the engineers they were working with. This led to the newly degreed person joining another company at an engineer's rate.

Later they were rehired at the first company at a rate comparable to peers with equivalent experience. Be sure the internal infrastructure of your company provides opportunities for those who do follow your policy for formal education appreciation or they will create their own system at the employer's cost.

Employees need to know what they can do specifically to improve their job performance. We need different skills to do different tasks, so why not leverage the strengths of your employees?

For some people, nothing is more frustrating than to be given a job but not the information needed to do it successfully. In one style of management, they tell the employee what not to do or not to repeat. The employee does the job again and it is wrong again so they have to be told again what they are doing wrong. This style of management is very passive aggressive and will frustrate employees.

Frustration has a physical impact on physical health. Kim Cameron's book *Positive Leadership* talks about research-based results that show heart rate changes, immune system suppression, hormone level changes and brain activity that shuts down in areas for creating solutions.

If the organization needs something new created, assign an employee with strengths in that area. Tell the employee what you want done, what the objectives are, and how they can successfully accomplish the task. Provide recognition and show genuine appreciation when they finish a job well done.

Appreciation has a physical impact on heart rhythm, strengthens the immune system, and lowers levels of stress chemicals in the body.

Work Case Scenario

Imagine that you are assigned to roll out a new initiative to be completed for your company before the end of the year, yet nobody tells you what the rest of the organization is doing. You ask people in your department what they have done so far and get vague responses because they don't know your technology platform, nothing is standardized, and they know only what they have done in their division or department. Compliance focuses on results because it is what the organization expects.

Then, before you can create a way to compare what they have done and what you need done, someone else announces that they are in charge of the Level 2 implementation of the same project. What you are doing may be a waste of time because compliance requires all locations to be at Level 2 by the first quarter of the next year. What would you think? How would you feel?

Some companies implement business plans this way. This causes a jaw drop response among employees. Some rise to the occasion and get to work but others wonder what's happening and ask themselves, "Whaaaat?!?" This could lead to employees reacting with a "Flight, Fright, Fight or Freeze (deer in the headlights)" response. There must be a better way.

Here is a different, healthier option. If technical initiatives are assigned to employees for implementation throughout the organization:

1. Provide an organizational status report with a timeline for the different stages of the project that have already been deployed

2. List names of who to contact and what their strengths are
3. Explain what has worked before
4. Show what has been a challenge so that each person does not need to spend enormous amounts of useless time and energy
5. If possible, use standardized systems or a global platform to streamline processes. Collaborative communication saves time.

Communication and learning from others in the organization can save time, reduce mistakes and create collaboration that streamlines implementation.

In many organizations, one department may not know what the other is doing because of ineffective communication. This lack of communication in most organizations is a luxury that they can no longer afford. Organizations aware of this challenge streamline communications and engage employees to strengthen their company.

Organizations that implement complex technology but don't streamline communication processes in advance find they spend hundreds of hours correcting problems. At times they discover that, unknown to management; individuals have implemented ideas that make their tasks easier. Some of these personal customizations are never discovered. If these adaptive insights are not shared, thereby making work better for everyone, you have missed an opportunity to save time and money.

In the book *Good to Great*, Jim Collins talks about how employee mindset differs between good companies and great companies.

Since his major premise is "Good is the enemy of Great," he says that some employees may not understand the impact they can have on an organization and will prefer Good practices that maintain the status quo versus long-term improvement toward greatness because they prefer the personal short-term benefits.

The decisions employees make every day reveal character. Be careful. If the system in place sends mixed messages and provides rewards for opportunistic personal behavior, you will confuse your employees, reduce morale, and hurt productivity because they will try to conform to the message you send.

In some cases, rather than offering a better solution the result could be that employees value a less than optimal system because they will get paid additional overtime. They rationalize that it's okay because management didn't plan and implement the project appropriately. The individual employee may also think that this is good because their skill at handling the problem seems to provide job security. This is not always the case.

In contrast, employee mindset in great organizations includes:

1. Employees have an effective and healthy way to work with management to implement processes correctly the first time and are rewarded through a safe environment.

2. Proactive communication corrects situations early in the process so that employee talents can be utilized in improving the organization in other ways.

If there isn't time to implement a process the correct way to begin with, when will there be time to correctly implement it? When employees see that they are valued for their insight, experience and hands on knowledge, they personally benefit, the company benefits and the customers they serve benefit.

When management is open to welcoming contributions from all employees, the better they will leverage the strengths of their talent and adapt in any market and on any technological platform.

To be authentic, employees in an organization must act as it says. If the organization's culture does not reflect what it professes to deliver, people will see the inconsistencies and doubt the integrity of the organization, its management, and the products it delivers.

Large companies like Enron, MCI, and the dotcoms failed when poor employee character and decision making processes were publicly revealed. The effects of these character revealing decisions were felt in the wallets of the shareholders and impacted millions beyond them.

Some employees who work from having a "job" perspective are transactional in nature. When an employee views their "career" contribution to the community there is a higher level of commitment, engagement and belonging to a group reflected in decisions they make in that organization. Employees, who see their work as a "calling," impart a higher level of meaning to their work and positive perspective in their role, and goals.

The size of the organization matters less than the character and personal perspectives of employees at all levels who make decisions on a daily basis. Employees who interact with their customers and see their value impacting others have higher levels of productivity, meaning and satisfaction. Decisions made by employees will eventually impact short- and long-term adaptive cycles that can result in the failure or the success of those businesses and impacts on the larger community.

Consider the following questions for your organization as you facilitate an authentic adaptation process for success:

- What types of decisions are supported in your organization and how?
- Is there a shared vision? Are decisions in the organization supported from results-aligned focus on the mission or do personal agendas detour them?
- When management is considering rolling out new programs, is there a shared vision including clear options and a process? Do you offer focus groups to collect input from employees? Does your organization implement programs and have people deal with problems on their own?
- Do you qualify the types of technology you need to support the organization's mission, values and behaviors? Do you ID Gaps or supporting infrastructure for employees and customers?
- What types of questions do you welcome or dislike in your organization from employees and from customers? Does this process lead to the continued health of the organization and its employees and foster constant improvement? Does this process hide or ignore something unhealthy that affects the organization in a systemic, toxic way. Is this the direction you want to go and if not what needs to be done to correct this?
- What missed opportunities could make your company more effective, productive, profitable, a better place for employees to work, and also for your customers to do business?
- Consider whether people are open to change or not. Do you want or need to get better? How healthy is your organization? Are they **Rigid** to the point of stunting healthy growth and possibly breaking or **Flexible** and open to new ideas?

In review:

Values and character, options, communication and collaboration will keep your organization adaptable during times of major challenge and change.

Remember to set clear practices, policies and procedures to serve as guidance to support behavior in service to the organization's mission. Reward strengths, good character and authentic behavior in your organizational talent.

Collaboration and building solid relationships in organizations will make it easier for everyone to care about others, have common goals, know others' strengths and feel empowered to act in challenging times and maintain their high performance in a positive environment.

Have options for Plan B, Plan C and so on because it is better to know what to do when the time comes rather than not know your options when problems strike.

Finally, communication is critical to the continued health of the organization, particularly when adapting to rapidly emerging needs, issues and concerns. Whether it includes current technology such as e-mail, Skype, user content videos, IP Video Conferencing, ISDN Video Conferencing, conference calls, webinar software, screen sharing or face to face, we need to feel comfortable with communication and technology and create that comfort for everyone.

Resources

Cameron, Kim (2010). *Positive Leadership: Strategies for Extraordinary Performance*

Collins, James, (2001). *Good to Great: Why Some Companies Make the Leap...and Others Don't*

Turban, Efraim and Leidner, Dorothy (2007). *Information Technology for Management: Transforming Organizations in the Digital Economy*

136 Adapt or Perish

17

The Succession Minded Employee
Lessons from the Military Model for Career Planning

By Murray Schrantz

Career Transitions for Military Personnel

When I left the military many years ago, the economy was robust and there was a strong demand for skilled workers, particularly those with a college degree.

Today's job market is a far different story, though the challenges of presenting valuable capabilities and experiences in a civilian context remain. For someone who was a mechanic in the Air Force, a nuclear technician in the Navy, or finance and accounting specialist in the Army, a similar job might seem to be an easy fit. Nonetheless, the business world operates in a different environment and speaks another language than the twenty-four hour military. Even a National Guard member or Reservist returning to a position that he or she left under a legal mandate that they be rehired may find that the old job has changed and the challenges to remaining successful are different. While the military does make some effort to prepare soldiers, Marines, and airmen for civilian life, it is woefully inadequate for anyone other than those seeking basic employment.

A career-minded individual will have to do exactly what the military trains them to do – understand the objective, acquire the skills necessary for success, and execute the plan aggressively. With that in mind, the primary challenge is to translate skills developed in the military into a format that the hiring authority for a civilian position will understand. They probably won't comprehend the mentality of dealing with IEDs, although they will understand the training and preparation, assessment of objectives and threats, ongoing vigilance, and proper planning to anticipate and resolve the problem.

Richard Bolles' *What Color is Your Parachute*[1] and its many revisions and updates is perhaps one of the most fundamental resources for job seekers. Despite the title, don't confuse this invaluable book with anything to do with the military. Though it may be tempting to skip to the end to see how it turns out, that strategy only works with *Harlequin* novels and *Star Trek* books. You must completely immerse yourself in the career development and job search information presented and complete the exercises to the best of your ability to make sure that your search is more than simply "finding a job, any job!" (For more on that subject, read John Hall's Chapter 28, *Adapt or Stagnate*).

Since most military personnel wear uniforms and most civilian employees do not (other than fast food franchise workers, police, firefighters, etc.), it's important to adapt to the environment where you'll be working. At an accounting firm or a law office, the dress standard will probably be a suit, though workers at a computer game developer may wear flip flops and tank tops.

Understanding this difference and the latitude of dress at each company is important to not sabotaging your chances when you first interview for the job. John Molloy's seminal book *Dress for Success*[2] has a wealth of information to help you sort through this process, though the specifics of the dress in vogue at the time of its writing are somewhat dated. The key is to assimilate into the new environment from a dress and appearance perspective. Setting your own style and getting recognized for your accomplishments and strengths will come later when differentiating yourself is important.

There are many benefits to spending 20 years or more in military service and having a regular retirement check (and other benefits) although many will leave after a only few years of service. In the same vein, one who has spent an entire career in the service of their country will likely have an even greater challenge understanding the opportunities and complexities of a career in the business world. In addition, there is the tradeoff between the valuable skill sets and experiences of a senior worker vs. younger workers (with the potential for a longer term relationship, lower starting salary and the vitality and energy of youth).

As an IT professional who wants more opportunities in IT or an MP who wants to become a police officer, you may have easier choices to make. For the rest of you, however (I was in the Infantry and had no aspirations to become a mercenary), the choices may not be so obvious and, even if they are, the path to a successful transition may not be as clear.

A large number of job search books are available on the market. The switch from a military environment to a civilian one, however, has its own set of challenges, like switching careers from Government to Corporate America or Non-Profits. On the other hand, there are true benefits to having experience in the Armed Forces that your peers on the outside will never experience (or perhaps understand). These skills, if presented properly to a prospective employer, can provide substantial advantages in the job search and retention process.

The focus of this chapter is to present suggestions and ideas to those leaving the service that help them better understand the value of their experiences.

This concept isn't novel, as described in the March 22, 2010 issue of *Fortune*[3] magazine, and corporate America has increasingly begun to take notice. Large multinational corporations have faced a growing problem with the looming retirement of millions of "Baby Boomers" and a lack of young leaders to replace them. Leaders and the transfer of leadership skills are needed in the global arena to remain competitive and relevant.

While that article focuses on opportunities for junior military officers, non-commissioned officers (NCOs) and the enlisted ranks can also provide a viable response to the rising vacuum in leadership. Though the active duty military may be the best source of needed skills, the Reserves and the National Guard are also potential incubators for meeting future requirements for the leaders of tomorrow. GE (an early leader in this effort), Wal-Mart, Home Depot, and Proctor and Gamble are examples of corporations that have long recognized the benefits of cultivating former military personnel in developing future leaders in their organizations.

Having established the existence of those opportunities, the next step is to define and present those skills unique to soldiers, sailors, and Marines in such a way as to distinguish you from your peers.

In this chapter, I will use the term "soldiers" as a generic description for all those who have served in any branch of the uniformed services (even Marines who prefer not to be lumped with the rest of us).

The value of military experiences is quite significant and includes the following:

- **Functioning in a team environment:** The military usually sets clear goals toward which the unit (division, fleet, air wing, etc.) strives. Those goals are clearly established and each subordinate unit and team member has one or more tasks that collectively support reaching that goal. The roles of each and the overall mission are defined in such a way that, ideally at least, everyone knows his or her requirements as well as those of their superiors to achieve their objective(s). If, due to casualties or other contingencies, individual or unit requirements change (as often happens), an appropriate response can be implemented to adjust for them and the mission continues.

- **Following policies, procedures, and orders while developing a creative approach to problem solving:** Training is seemingly a monotonous yet necessary aspect of military life that drills established procedures and protocol into both individuals and units to ensure that needed skills, equipment, and other vital assets are brought to bear in achieving the desired outcome. These abilities to act, rather than simply react, in an established manner in what might otherwise be a chaotic situation helps improve the chances for success. Fortunately, the military has "exercises" ("live fire" being the most exciting, dangerous, and expensive) to evaluate the effectiveness of training in a unified operation. The strong foundations of learning and application of principles in a creative and adaptive way for dynamic new environments is essential to attaining a successful outcome in business.

- **Working in a fast paced environment:** (how much more fast paced and urgent could it be than in combat?) – Outside the emergency medical field, few employees have to make split second life or death decisions (and even the former seldom requires that it be performed under fire) like police officers or sheriffs' deputies. This is where preparation and training, as previously described, are so vital to preparing for these exigencies.

- **Seeking opportunities for advancement:** The military has never been a static environment, even in peacetime. While the pace of change may slow when there is no open conflict, there is a continuing need to develop future leaders, create and expand secondary skills for contingencies, and to reinforce both the hard and soft skills needed to succeed. There is an "up or out" policy that ensures that no one stays as a clerk for their entire career. While specializations certainly exist, refining skills and developing leadership capabilities are a necessary mandate for all those in the military.

- **Learning to delegate appropriately** – All too often, when there is a perceived failure in business or society, Olympic caliber finger pointing may be the order of the day. Though not a perfect model, the policy of the military is that the leader is responsible for everything that happens or fails to happen under his or her command. This means that accountability not only exists for individuals but for functional units of operation as well. In corporate business, some companies refer to this as teams, project groups, programs, or divisions. Defining the resources needed to successfully complete the mission requires that a clear set of responsibilities be established and that everyone knows what is expected of them. A military maxim says that authority can be delegated but responsibility remains with the assigned individuals. In a business example, delegating authority to team members to create an effective display and presentation for a trade fair is a necessary part of the proper use of resources. The individual who has been given overall responsibility for its success must ensure that each person performs his or her function properly. If something is amiss, simply stating to the company leadership that Jim or Sally screwed up is pointless. The leader must take responsibility for the action of each member of the team.

- **Focused development of leadership capabilities** – Instead of leadership by committee or adopting the mantra that "if you can't be right, at least find someone to blame," leadership as a specific skill that is continually developed and practiced is a 'way of life' and is ongoing throughout the transition to corporate life. Regular practice with direct participation by the chain of command, supplemented by routine, formal evaluations to assess the capabilities and performance of individuals in meeting their objectives is required. Individuals are not appraised based primarily on their individual skills, but on their abilities to lead the efforts of their unit(s) to meet the objectives. This is not an abstract concept but rather an ongoing process of reinforcing essential strengths and implementing corrective actions to address less than optimal performance.

Understanding these qualities and processes is a necessary step in translating them into a meaningful and effective set of skills that differentiate you from your competition. Simply stating that you've had military experience or listing it in your resume hardly takes advantage of the proficiencies and expertise that you've spent long hours developing with self discipline. Many transitioning military personnel seldom give themselves enough credit for their experiences, especially when it comes to intangible traits such as team building, dealing with complexity and uncertainty, and working horizontally and vertically throughout most organizations. Likewise, stating that you've performed maintenance on an F/A-18E or spent the last year on a Virginia Class attack submarine doesn't convey your experience in terms that a hiring authority, much less a human resources department, will likely understand. The training, persistence, adaptation, and goal-oriented traits that were key to successfully reaching the many objectives inherent in military service, on the other hand, could be invaluable to potential employers.

Rather than describing in a resume or interview that you made E-5 in less than two years (a worthy achievement), it would be more appropriate to describe the requirements for that promotion (in civilian terminology) and how well you performed your duties in a way that could be easily understood by those outside the military. For example, instead of saying that you had "_ promotion points and were selected for below the zone promotion to SSG", it would be better to describe the skills that you developed to accomplish that goal, e.g. "acquired additional responsibility for … and achieved an 80% certification of those in my unit for the ___ and was promoted ahead of my contemporaries" (my Army experience reveals itself here, though it would be equally impressive to describe achieving high maintenance standards on mobile generators, proficiency with readiness drills on a littoral combat ship, etc.).

My co-author Dr. VaNessa Vollmer, who has assisted in helping military personnel successfully land jobs, has shared the following tips about this process:

1. **Lose the acronyms for your new resume.** This is a way to communicate faster while inside the military. However outside of an organization it takes this adaptation to succeed as an applicant. Translate what you did by describing it in terms of the job descriptions that you are considering applying for. After you are hired, you will most likely find new acronyms to learn and adapt to. On a resume to a recruiter, external acronyms look like alphabet soup.

2. **Assess your strengths.** Consider taking an assessment of your strengths (like Marcus Buckingham offers in his book *Go Find Your Strengths* or online). Knowing your strengths will be key to matching and leveraging them effectively for business needs. Sometimes people in business take a job because someone told them to be like their parents or it was the first thing that crossed their path, however later they may find themselves "in transition" or out of work because their interests or strengths did not align with their career. You may find it helpful to read Paul Tieger's *Do What You Are*. It helps individuals explore career options based upon their personality type (Myers Briggs self-evaluation). Consider this in the beginning of your search to get off on the right start.

3. **Once you know your strengths, consider your values.** There are many great values that arise from your experience serving

in the military. Write your personal core values down. When you search job websites, do your research and look for the company Mission Statement and Values. Compare your values with the company's and see if there is a "fit" or how comfortable you feel with those values and the Mission Statement. Look for signs of great ethics, leadership, transparency in communication, great customer service and people that value timeliness. If there is something that you are passionate about, like working with an organization that is aligning with environmentally safe practices, these are options to see what resonates with you and an organization of interest.

4. Some organizations, such as Aerospace, High Tech, IT or government, will seek out your expertise from the military. These are similar to what you have done or worked with before and some organizations will want your expertise. If you are a former pilot and they are looking to hire someone to assist in product development or program management because you know firsthand about what it is like to work with military products, this can be a great opportunity. For example, my Dad was in the Air Force and learned what parts worked well and which ones failed in the field. When he was hired by Hughes Aircraft from the Milwaukee School of Engineering, he utilized his education and field experience to design better products and that eventually help men land on the moon.

5. Smile! Relaxed hair trimming standards is another adjustment to get used to. Remember, in business people do business with people they trust and like. The self discipline, results process focus, timeliness and successful outcomes are all core skills and competencies that can shift into business and your new career.

6. Realize that this is an opportunity for new horizons, new adventures and for returning military to enjoy the country which they worked hard to protect. Successful adaptations in business and in your personal life will lead to quality performance as a way of life.

---

[1] *What Color is Your Parachute?* Richard Bolles
[2] *Dress for Success* John T. Molloy
[3] *Fortune* magazine, March 22, 2010

18

How to Work in a Virtual Organization

By Ilene Albert-Nelson

With the growth in virtual organizations, new opportunities open up for you as an employee. However, not everyone can work virtually and working virtually brings its own risks and rewards. Working virtually requires new skills and new ways of relating to your organization that you may not have today.

So what do you need to do to be successful as a virtual employee?

The most important thing is to rethink how you work. You won't have a time clock or your fellow workers to keep you on track. You won't have the casual interaction that you may be used to. But you will have more uninterrupted time to actually do your work as well as increased flexibility in your hours and how you approach your work time.

Here are some things to do if you work virtually:

- **Have a dedicated work space**. You need to have the mindset that you are still going to work even if you are just going to a home office. That means that you need a set space to work. And you shouldn't have your kids or your pets with you unless they are quiet. No one needs to know where you are or be subject to barking dogs or crying children, which is very unprofessional (and I have experienced both working with virtual employees).

- **Over communicate**. You may feel like you are spending too much time telling folks what you are doing or trying to stay synchronized with the team but it takes more communication to keep that level of synchronization if you are virtual. People don't see what you are doing, they don't see what you are accomplishing and they don't hear your voice in their day to day experience. So it is incumbent on you to make you and your work seen and heard.
- **Ask questions, don't assume.** Since you aren't there, you may not hear all the details of the plan. You may miss some information. It is important to ask even if you think you know the answer because you may not have the whole story.
- **Make sure you have regularly scheduled time with your manager.** You need a forum to review your work and for your manager to fill you in on information you may not be aware of given your virtual position. It is even more important to have this "face" time with your manager than it is when you are in the office
- **Request frequent team meetings so you and the team, who may also be virtual, can meet and share.** It helps for everyone to hear information at the same time and to share what they know. This meeting helps take the place of the casual interactions you might normally have.
- **Develop relationships with the rest of the team.** The team is your strength and if you pool what you know, you will be stronger. If you are all working virtually, it is entirely possible that one or more of you will have information that can help the rest. Remember that as you learn things, you don't have the casual office learning environment to share so you have to build an even stronger esprit de corps with the team to share learning and information.
- **Use an instant messenger program so you have real time communication and can avoid phone tag.** (You may also want to use Skype or other video internet phone methods.) There is

no replacement for real time communication. If you have a quick question or want to share something, it is fast and easy to instant message. It also avoids a lot of phone tag. If you are on the phone with a customer, it is a way to get answers just like someone was sitting next to you and you could lean over and ask. I have found instant messenger to be a very powerful team tool when working virtually.

- **Ask to be in the office or to have other face to face time with the entire team at some set schedule per year.** You still need the face time. You should make an effort to get into the office so you can be seen and heard on a regular basis. It helps if your company is willing to get the team together whether it is at the office or at a trade show or other event. Being virtual means you have to make an effort to be present and be seen and heard.

- **Don't take communication gaps personally**: no one is out to get you or determined to keep you in the dark (see communicate above). It is very easy for someone to forget to tell you something that you need to know. You may also not know who the right contact is in the organization. Get over the feeling of being deprived or hurt – it is highly unlikely that these oversights are deliberate; it is much more likely that you are out of sight and therefore out of mind. You need to not let your feelings get involved; but make sure your manager is aware of the information that you need and that something wasn't communicated.

Being a virtual employee can be a great experience and a great way to work for a company that is in another geographic area. It is also a terrific opportunity if you want more flexibility in your work day. Using these simple tactics can help you be more successful and feel more like a part of the team even without being in the office.

148 Adapt or Perish

19

The Challenge of Managing Virtual Organizations

By Ilene Albert-Nelson

In my last role, I managed 18 people in seven locations. Only four people were in the same office I was. This doesn't include vendors in Asia or outside sales reps. (We had eight groups of outside reps). Managing a virtual organization isn't for the faint of heart or for those who like a lot of control over their subordinates. It takes more effort and a high communication level to maintain. It doesn't work in all organizations and cultures. It isn't easy. But it is a growing trend and odds are that at least part of your organization may become virtual if it isn't already.

Virtual organizations are a fact of life in business today. With technology at its current level, it has become possible for people to work remotely in roles outside of sales (where working remotely has always been more likely). More and more people aren't willing to relocate to work for your organization but you want them for their skills. This is also a function of acquisitions where the talent resides in another location and your company doesn't want to lose the skills, relationships and tribal knowledge. (Acquisitions were part of the way

I ended up with some of the disparate locations that I was managing and the skills that people had were skills we needed to retain.) Many companies now have offices in China or other locations for production reasons even if they are smaller companies.

Flat Earth by Thomas Friedman says that virtual is the future. There are many tools to link people to organizations beyond cohabitating in the same office.

Let's look at some of the current statistics on telecommuting:

- The number of Americans who worked from home or remotely at least one day per month for their employer (employee telecommuters) increased from approximately 12.4 million in 2006 to 17.2 million in 2008. A 39% two-year increase and 74% increase since 2005. (WorldatWork Telework Trendlines 2009)
- Gartner Dataquest reports that in 2008 25% of workers telecommuted in 2007 and the 2009 projection was 27.5%.
- Relocating for a new job hit a record low in the first quarter of 2008 of 8.9% according to Challenger, Gray & Christmas. They are seeing a return to relocating in early 2009 but still not the historic norms and nowhere near the levels of the 1990s and 2000s.

How do you manage an organization in all four US time zones? What are the specific challenges and new skills that are needed to do this? This chapter won't cover all the different tools that are available but will talk about management skills, some of the communication tools and tool types and considerations for managing virtual organizations.

The Challenges for Managers

No casual "in the hall" communication

You don't realize how much business is done by casual, impromptu conversation until you don't have your folks around to do this. A virtual organization requires more awareness that you must share and communicate in a structured way to make things work. You may feel like you are in the middle of playing the old telephone game as you have to tell multiple people the same stories. And no, email doesn't solve the problem. Email is also too structured and many people don't or can't communicate well in email. Many people are much harsher in email. You lose the nuances and the ability to deal with problems lightly when you put it in writing.

Not strongly linked to company culture

All the folks who are working in another office or at home aren't part of the everyday communication and interaction that creates the company culture. Another office develops their own culture and it takes on the culture of the people who work there, which could be radically different from what you want. People who work from home have no work culture. Why does this matter? Because how your company addresses and solves problems, how you work together and communicate and what the culture does and doesn't tolerate may be unknown to your virtual organization. This leads to unintended consequences including tonality that rubs people the wrong way. Plus, they don't know who to ask certain questions of and little things can start to loom very large.

Not part of the informal grapevine that makes companies work

Don't kid yourself – the grapevine is how new employees learn who is who and what is what. The virtual person isn't connected and may never figure out the unwritten rules. They don't have the advantage of hearing the "scuttlebutt" that greases the wheels of every organization.

May not be involved in company events

This is one of those little things that mean a lot to people. Having a company holiday lunch? What about holiday gifts? They aren't in the office so they tend to be forgotten and it is these little things that make people feel part of the team and appreciated.

Feeling alone and unloved

Your virtual employees may miss critical information because they weren't part of a conversation or you have round robin conversations that end up more like a game of telephone with the end person having a totally different and unintended story.

This is one of the most important and hardest parts of managing a virtual organization. You want people to have time to do their jobs and not schedule large structured team meetings all the time. But without this, you will have the same conversation multiple times and everyone may hear something differently. Plus your virtual staff may have conversations of their own.

How To Avoid The Pitfalls: Skills To Make Virtual Work
Communicate, communicate, communicate!

You may feel like you are over-communicating but odds are you aren't! Communication is the biggest and most important challenge that you will have. Here are some tools and techniques to address this:

1. **Weekly scheduled time with every team member and scheduled sub-team meetings.** Discipline in scheduling and getting on the phone with people both individually and as a team is critical. Your virtual folks need to feel connected and need to know what you know. Since you don't have the informal communication method available, you have to have the discipline to create the opportunities for your organization to have time with you and each other to foster that team culture and make sure that everyone is on the same page.

2. **Real time communication tools such as Yahoo Messenger.** I am not advocating Yahoo IM instead of others such as Microsoft or Google. But it is handy and powerful to message in real time. Even if it is just to find out if someone is available to take a call or to ask a quick question, instant message tools are as close as you can get to popping into someone's office. I used IM extensively and found it was highly valuable for fostering communication and team cohesiveness. IM also allows people to let their personalities show much better than email. Instant messages also avoid the round robin and copying that occurs with email. Email is not a real time tool!

3. **Real time collaboration tools such as Google Groups, Google Wave, and Central Desktop.** These programs allow you to share documents and track conversations among a team. Large companies may have their own on-line collaboration tools but if you are a smaller company these tools help people with large projects that need to be shared share them. Sending things via email means that multiple people are saving different versions of documents and may not remember to copy everyone who wants or needs to see the project docs.

4. **Internet video and Skype.** Nothing makes up for being able to see people's faces and reactions. Silence on the phone can mean a lot of things! Your company may struggle with the bandwidth but it saves a lot of travel money if you can meet virtually. Large companies have teleconference equipment but the rest of us can do it for free or for little money. If you have a laptop, odds are it has a built in camera and Skype is free!

5. **Regularly scheduled team conference calls.** The only way to build team esprit de corps and culture is to create regular communication. Let your staff recommend the topics. Let the team own the call but have it!

6. **Regularly scheduled face to face time.** I spent a lot of time on planes. As the manager, you need to be able to see your team on a regular basis. Try to see everyone at least quarterly. You can mix who comes to corporate and who you need to go see. There is a certain amount of "prestige" for your virtual folks to coming to the corporate office no matter how small that office is. This is where the decisions are made and the people they rely on live. Make the effort to meet or the resentments will build. You do not want your staff to feel neglected.

7. **Management travel to remote offices of cities where people are clustered.** One of the things your virtual organization misses is seeing the CEO, President or other senior executives. They don't hear the company meetings or updates and have no exposure. Exposure is critical to people's careers so the more you can get your management out to meet them or bring your virtual organization to the corporation, the more integrated they will feel and the easier your conversations with senior management will be. Remember, if management hasn't met your folks then they are faceless cogs in the wheels of the organization and it may lead to decisions being made that may not be in the best interests of your team or your people.

8. **Commitment from ALL team members to make the virtual team work.** It takes a lot of work from the whole team to make a virtual organization work. Everyone has to learn to communicate in new and different ways and to speak up when necessary even if that may not be their preference. The issues of being part of a virtual team are addressed in Chapter 18, How to Work in a Virtual Organization.

When a Virtual Organization Doesn't Work

Virtual organizations aren't for every company, manager or person. You can see how challenging they are to manage and how the entire organization has to be willing to support it. Here are some of the things that will defeat a virtual organization:

1. **Management doesn't support it.** Not all management teams or managers want to have people who aren't right there in the office. They may not trust what they can't see (are these people really working?), they may feel that they don't have enough control (what are they doing anyway?) or they may feel that it doesn't foster team and culture (this is the toughest objection!). Regardless of the reason, if your senior management doesn't support it or understand it, you are destined to fail.

2. **Remote workers become too dysfunctional.** Your organization may not be able to handle remote workers depending on the type of work and company culture. They can be resented and, since they aren't part of the everyday presence, they can be ignored or brushed off. Your organization may find remote workers just too hard. Conversely, your remote workers can create problems since they may not understand the unwritten rules of how things work. They are perceived as loose cannons or not part of the larger team. When this happens, that person or the idea of remote workers may need to be changed.

3. **Not everyone is cut out to work remotely**. It can be difficult to be cut off from your co-workers, hard to get yourself motivated and hard to be disciplined about actually working if you are home. Some people miss being where the action is and aren't organized or disciplined enough to work on their own.

So Would I Do It Again?

Virtual organizations have their place in the world of corporations and they aren't going to go away but will continue to grow. I would do it again to hire the right talent or have the right person in the right location (for a customer, vendor etc.) or allow someone to be more successful in their job (this is the world of people who only come to the office part of the week). Yes, it is a management challenge but you can have a strong successful virtual team!

20

Music, Nature and Successful Organization Commonality

By VaNessa Vollmer

Good news produces statements like, "Wow, that's music to my ears."

Although music is pleasing to hear, this statement refers to another fact about music: It takes a lot of practice to become a fine musician and play well with other musicians. Like all other skills, musicians need a strong knowledge of fundamentals before they can build new musical variations like classical, jazz, rock and roll, blues, new wave, and punk. By creating these variations, musical artists give us new insights into the human experience.

What do musicians, nature and successful organizations have in common?

This question is rarely asked since most people would not recognize the common principles if asked. However, when we do consider this question, we learn how to make our organizations more successful by leveraging their natural strengths. Some facets that both musicians and successful organizations share are:

- Learn the basics

- Build knowledge through experience from implementing and practicing fundamentals
- Reflect on experiences
- Create questions for mentors. Receive answers and insights that eventually evolve into expertise
- Achieve new levels of excellence.

In every trade or career you will find examples of how this process leads to excellence.

Skill	Music	Nature	Organization
Learn the Basics	Language, Tuning notes	Language Names	Language Business
Build Knowledge	Learn, Practice	Learn, Interactions	Learn Knowledge, Skills
Reflect on Experience	Works Well for Improvements Tone, Technique	Successful or Perishes	Constants Improvements or fix what didn't work
Create Questions for Mentors and Leaders	Guidance offered for areas of concern from conductor or section heads.	Learn "Why" some things work better	Learn vicariously what you can do better from previous experience. Use coaches, mentors to learn from.
Accomplish Excellence	Excellent Performances	Survival of the Fittest	Increased performance, innovation, profits and business excellence.

In music, there are different sized groups: solos, duets, quartets, chamber music, and bands or symphonies that focus on classical music. Musical groups have a variety of instruments and vocals that determine the dynamic result. Possibilities include cultural music variation.

Instrumental basics involve language acquisition, tuning, learning notes and fundamentals for how to play. Musicians will practice alone, in sections and in the band or orchestra as a whole. Practice behaviors differ depending on what the musician is practicing. However, no musician or musical group would ever consider performing without tuning together first because they would sound terrible and the purpose is to make great music. Alone, a musician will concentrate on building individual skills and improvisation ability to become more advanced and comfortable in the role or performing as a soloist. When musical groups rehearse separately in sections, they practice working together as a unit, get to know the difficulty of the composition, and master their parts as a group.

When the full group rehearses, it tunes instruments together. The conductor provides another set of ears and works on blending all of the sections into a whole that sounds better than the separate sections. The conductor will also stop the group from playing a piece if they are out of sync or play the wrong notes, then coach them by humming the right ones if needed in rehearsal.

Some musical groups help each other by checking for tone and tuning in different weather environments. The more they play music together, the more they notice and anticipate what types of situations, like how cold or heat, affect other instruments and make tuning adjustments to correct the difference, making everyone sound great.

Seasoned and well rehearsed musicians realize that everyone needs a break, including leaders. When high levels of mastery are achieved, the musicians can play together even without a conductor. For instance, at a football game, when a score is made musicians pick up their instruments and play the team's song whether the leader is present or not. They understand their role, are "self led" and don't skip a beat!

When musicians tune first, then practice, practice, practice, they create harmony and the results are music to our ears (usually). Just like music, nature has basic, group, and improvisational systems.

Nature has many different systems but to simplify it, growing a plant requires three basics: growing medium, water and light. If there are no nutrients in the growing medium, the plant will not grow. If the plant does not use the nutrients effectively, it will weaken and die.

Nature has a logical proposal, do this and live or don't and die. If the goal is to survive and thrive, then you need to figure that out in time to adapt before you perish.

If the goal is to survive, strengthen and flourish, then there is a process that involves understanding your role in the environment, creativity, natural problem solving, and taking action to adapt. When nature provides the right amounts of everything plants need to survive, they will thrive and produce new growth and seeds for future generations.

Organizations expect their employees to have the appropriate knowledge, skills and abilities to do their job well. If these are at a lower level than the organization needs, then like the plant that needs nutrients it may not succeed. The organization must encourage employee enrichment. Training enriches employees' natural growth experiences.

Coaches and mentors supplement employee enrichment for expertise and leadership roles. Enriched resources are required if employees and organizations are going to thrive and adapt in the changing business environment. If another plant blocks sunlight in the growing area, the life in that area needs to adapt to lower light levels or seek new energy sources. In the same way, organizations seek energy sources to produce products and services and reap a return on their investment.

Organizations need to know the strengths of their employees, enrich those strengths, and effectively leverage them for successful growth and profits.

It is curious that some organizations under-invest in this process. How many of you are in organizations that don't know what their employee strengths are?

Many have seen organizations do reorganizations; however do decision makers consider employee strengths or base the changes on politics and personal agendas?

If reorganizations are politically or ego-based personal agendas, it becomes as apparent in the same way a musical group would if it switched to instruments the performers don't play right before the performance. Sounds awful, right? You might think no one would do this; however we've seen or heard it happen and seen the unfortunate results.

On the other hand, some organizations take employee strengths in knowledge, skills and abilities into consideration and support employee growth. Just as some musicians learn to play more instruments, they use bridge core skills in this new role like tuning, reading music, and playing their new instrument's part in the group.

Constructive professional development, organizational needs and adapting to changes in the business environment need to be well planned, strategic and supported by enriched resources.

Invent, Design and Implement Innovation

There are several classic management principles. Power functions best in a self organized, equitable, malleable, and cooperative system.

Consider specialization, standardization, plans and control. Hierarchies include primacy of intrinsic and extrinsic rewards. Each segment of the organization community looks at change and asks, "What's in it for me?" The answer is different for everyone.

Once the organization masters these basic management principles, it and its units can find new management principles that work well in specific situations. This is the essence of innovation and adaptation, building from the known to the unknown.

Three key considerations for creating innovation are:

1. What areas currently exhibit the qualities that you'd like to have in your organization?
2. Where do you find those traits and desirable qualities in the current entity?
3. How can you get desirable qualities throughout your organization?

For example, your company is as agile as change itself so it is highly adaptable. Continuous strategic renewal to accommodate change can be a challenge for large organizations unless their culture has adaptability imbued in their corporate culture. Some parts of the organization will be better at this than others.

Classic Management Principles

Natural systems adapt over years, decades, or centuries through genetic innovation. Decision making is based on what survives. "Evolv-ability" is the key to change and adaptation. In nature, old processes remain but are repurposed and used a new way.

A grocery store can make a change like going from using paper bags to plastic bags. When it is discovered that plastic bags have an effect on the environment, a new opportunity arises to create a better, profitable, and innovative product.

Some organizations over-invest in the past and under-invest in the future, which can harm the long term success of the organization. The comment, "This is the way that we've always done it," may be true, however your competitors will not think the same way.

The two questions become: Is our future success based on the same ideas that we've built our past success on? Or do we create new ideas for future success while we leverage our legacy products?

If the organization opts for the first method, it risks losing customers. "Head in the sand" thinking may feel comfortable but creates the same bleak vision for the future because the company still faces the risk that the world will change in spite of what it does, leaving it far behind in the competitive race.

Leadership and Decision Making

In Greek mythology, Procrustes had a bed he rented out to visitors. To make the person fit, he used a very simple procedure: If the person was too short for the bed, he stretched them to fit. If the person was too tall, he lopped off part of their body to make them fit. The goal was simple: to make the person fit!

This simple process doesn't take much in-depth reasoning skill to get results.

Unfortunately, oversimplification may get the job done but creates immense collateral damage. Understanding a problem takes more time and energy and reduces damage but also reduces over-simplification as in Occam's Razor, where the simplest solution is best. However, if you cut out too much data valuable information will be lost. It is an art that involves critical thinking skills and careful reference to statistics. The convention of making decisions based on oversimplification and flippant communication stifles innovation.

Adversarial leadership tends to oversimplify and place power in the hands of a very few top executives. Innovation does not thrive in environments like this. Even though it is more difficult to create, giving a sense of power to individuals and sections in organizations is a far more powerful way to foster innovation. Leaders who use role modeling and mentoring with personal and professional growth create cohesive groups.

Effective leadership is necessary to unlock this transformational process. When employees understand what their role is within the organization and know the desired results, connecting the dots will deliver outstanding service to internal customers and earn admiration from external customers.

People like and feel good about working in an empowering organization that facilitates internal and external success. Leaders guide employees to successful results, client and customer needs are met, and the company grows.

When they incorporate other people's interests into the process, companies benefit from feedback and are more likely to succeed in the long term. New employees and new customers see this, learn from this mission, and institute best practices that empower greatness.

When we learn from others to use processes that work, it makes life easier. Why not enjoy these gifts and share them with others?

Business books such as *Good to Great* by Jim Collins share valuable common lessons that if implemented result in understanding greatness and genuine peace of mind. *Positive Leadership* by Kim Cameron gives insights that help you recognize and leverage positive deviant performance as successful adaptations for your organization. When others see chaos or things that don't work, positive deviants see opportunistic solutions. They understand the system, how situations occur, and how this relates to solutions.

David Rock's book, *Your Mind at Work*, clarifies a natural neuroleadership supported from the molecular level of thought processes to behavior that empowers creativity, builds better relationships and enhances performance.

When leaders trigger a threat response, employees' brains become much less efficient because fear makes them lose focus. Good leaders:

1. Make people feel good about themselves
2. Clearly communicate their expectations
3. Give employees latitude to make decisions
4. Support people's efforts to build good relationships
5. Treat the whole organization fairly

These actions prompt a rewarding response for everyone involved. Others in the organization become more effective, more open to ideas, and more creative.

Why fight the brain when you can successfully leverage natural strengths for your organization? Natural thought processes determine what messages leaders send to their organizations, whether it is musical or natural-based business. Some people won't understand and think only of themselves.

Narcissists don't make great leaders, according to Seth Godin in his book *Linchpin* and Daniel Goleman agrees in his book *Primal Leadership*. Goleman emphasizes this in his story of Dunlap, which made decisions based on fear and authoritarian power. Who needs this negative effect in their company when it threatens people, avoid sresponsibility and ultimately stifles profits and performance?

Keep your leadership vision clear and communicate it throughout the organization and understand your internal and external customers. When you conduct business, you want to make sure that everyone is playing the same music, on the same page with their instrument of mastery, and will perform with transformational excellence. If you do this, your employees and organization will experience mastery, elevated performance, and thrive. Satisfied customers return.

Heed their wisdom as they pay you to perform because customers will tell you what they want. If you give it to them, they will be back for more, and another encore!

The survival of the fittest is the ageless law of nature, but the fittest are rarely the strong. The fittest are those endowed with the qualifications for adaptation, the ability to accept the inevitable and conform to the unavoidable, to harmonize with existing or changing conditions.
~Dave E. Smalley

Resources

Cameron, Kim S. (2008). *Positive Leadership: Strategies for Extraordinary Performance*
Collins, Jim (2001). *Good to Great: Why Some Companies Make the Leap and Others Don't*
Godin, Seth (2010) *Linchpin: Are You Indispensable?*
Goleman, Daniel (2004). *Primal Leadership: Learning to Lead with Emotional Intelligence*
Rock, David (2009). *Your Brain at Work: Strategies for Overcoming Distraction, Regaining Focus, and Working Smarter All Day Long*
Zaffron, Steve and Logan, Dave (2009). *The Three Laws of Performance: Rewriting the Future of Your Organization and Your Life*

21

Finding Unique Solutions

By Steve Amos

Most people are problem solvers. How do you stretch and become a truly great problem solver? This is a how to chapter. If I had to simplify the article, it is well stated in the following quote: "A problem well stated is a problem half solved." – Charles Kettering

How to Solve Any Problem

If you do not have any problems, you can skip this article. Notice that everyone is still reading. Why? Life is full of problems. We encounter them daily in business and in our personal lives. How we handle problems often dictates how others perceive us, our position, and how much we earn.

Here is how to successfully solve any problem:

Really Want to Resolve It

Most people say, "Wouldn't it be nice if this went away." So to resolve a problem you have to be ready to change. You will experience obstacles and failures. It will take time and effort and will upset somebody to solve your problem. It can upset you to solve your problem. To fix anything, someone has to change what they or you are doing. There is a natural resistance to change that does not go away easily. We have all said, "That's the way we always do it" at some point in our lives.

Why is it a Problem?

Who does it bother? Your customer, your coworker, your boss, your significant other, or is it you who are bothered? Why are they bothered? Once you have identified the problem, you can do something about it.

What are the Causes?

What caused your problem? Are these causes clear and why do they exist? Are these causes rooted in tasks created for some other now forgotten reason? The secret is to track down these root causes then break down the variables that affect your problem. Then you can change the variables to see if you can find a solution. This is the "Black Box" analysis technique engineers use daily.

What Changed?

This shortcut can be used to find the source of the problem. If something was working before and now doesn't work, this question will often identify the cause. However if something previously worked poorly, there was no change and this question solves very little. Use caution to ensure that going back is worthwhile. The best solutions may lie ahead instead.

Ask Everyone Involved for Their Input.

Those closest to the problem have the best insights to what is wrong. They ferret out the roots of the problem. Often the answer comes from the person least likely to know the solution. Be open-minded about who can help.

Describing a problem to someone helps define it. It's a simple, fast and effective way to analyze problems. Two heads or more are usually better than one.

The goal is to correctly define the problem before proposing solutions. You would be surprised how much time is spent solving the wrong problem, often by very senior and experienced people. How do I know this? Experience.

Finding Solutions

Now that the problem is defined, it is time to find solutions. The best approach is to find as many solutions as possible. Don't stop at the first one that sounds good. "For every complex problem, there is a solution that is simple, neat, and wrong." – Henry Louis Mencken.

Where does creativity come from? It comes from mixing unrelated concepts and opposites. Take all the ideas and combine different solutions to create better results. Put coffee shops in bookstores. Make long shorts. Bring the repair shop to the customer.

The best solution seems obvious after you find it, but it takes a lot of work to put it together.

Stay with it

The first attempt at anything is rarely successful. Try and try again is the only way to solve anything. Solving a problem is often done with stubbornness as much as with talent. Refuse to quit. Be bullheaded. Solutions don't require a college degree. The experience will make you a more talented problem solver.

Thomas Edison had over 900 failures before he succeeded in creating the light bulb. Problem solvers don't give up.

Look for others who have a similar problem

Industry, professional, and self-help groups are often great sources of ideas for how to attack a problem. Look at outside industries for better ideas that you can adapt to your industry. American industry lost a great lead on the rest of the world by not taking others' ideas. Call it the "Not Invented Here" syndrome.

Try different problem solving techniques

History is full of companies (and people) that found a solution for customers, blossomed, and then died as changes left them behind. Don't be a One Trick Pony. Learn how other problem solvers succeed and try it yourself. Don't be afraid to start with small changes. Success builds further successes. Kaizen has been extremely successful for manufacturers and designers for decades.

To innovate is rare and takes serious effort. Change the rules. Don't compete but reinvent the game to own the higher ground.

"Anyone can make the simple complicated. Creativity is making the complicated simple." -Charles Mingus

Analyze the consequences

What effects will different solutions have? Solutions need to be evaluated before they are implemented. For instance, starting a war may leave your country's economy and military ruined. Diplomacy may be a better solution to try first.

Once you evaluate the alternatives, prioritize the possible answers.

Test your solution

What consequences will your solution have? Try to model the smallest piece of your problem and see if it works. Listen carefully to any feedback. Do not take the griping that comes with the feedback personally. Just ferret out the facts.

If your solution fails to work, refer to "Stay With It." Experience always has value.

Sell your solution

Now you think there is a solution. You must overcome resistance to change. Most of this resistance arises when people are told to do something without a reason. If you can explain the reason clearly, your solution is more likely to succeed. My experience is that solutions are rarely accepted the first time they are explained. Generally people need a minimum of three or four exposures to a new idea before they accept it. Often marketing will take dozens of exposures to get a new customer to try your product or service. Don't give up.

Risk taking is a normal part of business. The biggest risk takers like stunt men and athletes prepare carefully for events we consider potentially dangerous. We need to do the same for our businesses.

Give credit to those who helped you

People will be more likely to help you in the future if you have established a track record of not taking all the glory. Everyone has to pull together to succeed. You will get your share of the credit, partner.

Conclusion

Persistence and patience are necessary to solve any problem. Practice and experience will make it easier as you go along. Don't give up. After you succeed, find your next problem to solve.

22

Creating Teams in Corporate Communities

By VaNessa Vollmer

I was fortunate to have a college instructor plant an idea in my mind when I was younger. He said, "...if you observe people carefully you will learn that there are individuals that will be able to accomplish and create great things in this world. However, if you look closer you will find that when people work well together, they can create something better than one person alone."

My understanding has grown since then as I continued to observe and learn from people. To test this idea, I researched many brilliant minds and their accomplishments over the years, which confirmed that it is very insightful and useful. One key way this idea worked effectively was when people acknowledged their own strengths and the strengths of people they worked with. This sparked everyone's imagination, stimulated intelligent change throughout the team and the organization, and led to accomplishing the goal.

Knowledge workers want practical tools and useful information to aid their professional development and business accomplishments. They need new models that help them grab business opportunities for their team and their organization. When given these tools, every member of the team thinks bigger and better, produces more innovative ideas, and works more intelligently with others to create synergy.

Research suggests that practical applications based on Learning Theory acknowledge a worker's need for encouragement, a support system, and recognition.

Brain activity changes based on feedback you get. Supportive visualization of goals, encouragement, and acknowledgment of successful improvement reflects chemical changes in the brain that encourages learning and mastery.

While there are different learning opportunities: informal, on the job, formal through training or coaches and mentors, successive steps toward success can serve as a reward.

One to one Learning with a coach or mentor is common and constructive involving six phases:

1. Mentor and employee are introduced and get to know each other.
2. Mutual trust develops because they work and learn from each other, a type of basic reciprocity.
3. Mutual risk taking is encouraged by the mentor for the employee to grow and learn more.
4. Mentor and employee understand each other better and anticipate and create new learning opportunities.
5. The employee shifts to a more dominant role in the process as they move toward mastery.
6. The employee practices from the lead role perspective and the relationship with the mentor adapts to a colleague at the same level.

The success of a mentor or coach requires that the coach have the skills needed to make the transfer, the ability to transfer and teach others to master the same skills, and determine specific, clear outcomes. Not every expert has the ability to teach others and some are intolerant or critical, which can do more damage than good. It is best to offer face to face time and insure that programs are voluntary and that relationships are not forced on mentors or employees.

Thank goodness strong leaders are comfortable surrounding themselves with other competent knowledge workers like themselves.

Companies today are shifting away from doing the same things they have done in the past. Bernard Bass distinguished between transactional versus transformational leaders. Transactional Leaders are more traditional in the sense of influencing subordinates to insure that agreed performance levels are met. Emotionless transactions take place to take care of business. In contrast, Transformational leaders inspire and leverage intellectual stimulation and individual driven interests to transform and enrich employee experiences.

Transformational leaders facilitate elevated interest areas and develop employees. More organizations realize that just transactions for conducting business may get business done, however changes in the global market require further consideration of benefits from transformational leadership for long term business success.

Why would you want employees to come to work just for a paycheck when the option exists for enthusiastic employees who are engaged, contribute in business and creatively offer better business solutions? They find that it is better to ask questions and then alter practices to those that lead to innovations. Slight changes in corporate cultures make the difference between companies that remain viable in the marketplace versus those who champion it!

First, they need to assess what customers want. Second, they need to look at how and why they conduct business and what else they can do to serve customers and cope with rapid change in the marketplace, which is changing from local to global due to growth technologies like the Internet.

Successful companies are changing the systems they use to create more enjoyable ways to do business, serve customers, and meet their needs. Some companies have underutilized resources like employees. The employees of most organizations have great ideas but many companies have no way to tap into these ideas to improve products, profits and innovation.

Companies that use input from their employees will lead the global market when they implement these ideas.

Many organizations say that people are their greatest resource, yet how to tap into what their employees have to offer is still a mystery for them. It is a blip on the organizational radar that goes unnoticed and unquestioned.

Transformation can facilitate change at the individual level and at the group level, which includes departments, divisions or the entire organization. In a community system, it can empower cities, counties, states, and nations.

Changes begin and happen with a shared vision. The company decides on the business results they need to succeed. How you implement the process that gets you there can be accomplished a few different powerful ways.

The power of leadership can be qualified into five types:

1. **Reward Power**: based on the ability to provide rewards for great performance.
2. **Coercive Power**: relates to the ability to punish like when someone is written up or fired.
3. **Legitimate Power**: relates to the position within the organizational hierarchy like a supervisory role.
4. **Referent Power**: based on admiring or liking the person because the employee identifies with that leader.
5. **Expert Power**: results from expertise and skills in a specific knowledge area.

The three listed first are found in position power and the last two are based in personal relating power. Yukl and Falbe's research shows the last two categories are the most important reasons for complying with leadership requests.

Since employees tend to pay more attention to negative consequences, it is important to understand that coercive power is negatively associated with satisfaction. Coercive Power is more commonly found in competitive organizational cultures or relationships.

Employees want to avoid punishment and in some cases are dissatisfied and resent being told what to do, especially when they know there is a better way to accomplish a business goal. This type of employee tends to do better in collaborative organizations when leadership has healthy egos and includes them in business processes as part of the team.

When this type of employee is involved in the processes and leadership announces "this is the way that it is going to be" and hears their ideas were included in the plan, this increases morale, employee engagement, and makes them feel like they have a part in the organization's success. By communicating the results of this inclusion process, the vision transforms into a more powerful, shared goal. Everyone needs to feel involved in the process as a stakeholder so that they can all be part of the group and on the same page for success.

Consistent communication is key for this inclusive model. The need to reassure people that the plan will work takes a back seat when employees participate and clearly understand what needs to be accomplished. When re-gearing and training are necessary, provide resources and facilitate opportunities to acquire knowledge, skills and abilities to create continued success.

There are organizations that embrace this innovative process to the extent where they have teams or individuals work on projects for "24 hours" straight. These projects can be related to their current projects or completely different. The only goal during this time is that they must deliver something "overnight." As a result, employees in this company have developed new products, huge customer pleasers and breakthrough technology! Add momentum by celebrating project successes and renew development to reinforce the organizational shift toward the goal. If people become overwhelmed by the size of a project, break it into chunks people can deal with comfortably. This way, people will know how to contribute to the organization's success at the team and individual level. See what extraordinary results you achieve with your employees and your business. This process works because of the intrinsic thrills your employees feel from learning, creative freedom, autonomy, and accomplishment.

Employer Magnetism

As an employer, you need to become a magnet that attracts people who want to help make your shared vision happen. Facilitate the process to design the culture and organize your plan so that you become an employer of choice. The company's brand will attract people because they want to be a part of your organization because they embrace similar values, core beliefs, and supportive behaviors.

Another key aspect of developing your successful teams and organization is an ongoing skills inventory. You need assessments to discover and quantify skill gaps that need to be filled to develop employees, grow leadership and create cultural competency.

The wise organization in the current market will know how to compete for talent. It will know what it does better than other companies and will commit to this as part of its brand.

Companies brand from the inside, through employees or people within the community, creating a synergistic effect that improves the companies' image and performance.

The internal beliefs of the members are the key to making this happen. Believing that the goal will happen, acquiring the knowledge about what has worked in the past and why, and what has not worked in past and why, helps a company avoid pitfalls and facilitates the change process that creates better products and services.

You need to ask yourself these questions:

1. Do you really want to get better at something? (Because some people say they do but really don't, so be honest with yourself and others.)
2. Are you willing to entertain something different?

If the answer to both of these questions is "Yes" then consider this:

Find someone who has successfully done what you would like to do and ask them to mentor or coach you. Why put off being a better person, a better organization, part of a better community, or even a better world?

References

Cameron, Kim (2008). *Positive Leadership: Strategies for Extraordinary Performance*

Godin, Seth (2007). *The Dip: A Little Book That Teaches You When to Quit (and When to Stick)*

Honold, Linda (2001). *How to Promote Learning at Work: Developing Employees Who Love to Learn*

Pink, Daniel (2009). *Drive: The Surprising Truth About What Motivates Us*

Seidman, William and McCauley, Michael (2009). *Strategy to Action in 10 Days: Creating High Performance Organizations*

Section 3

Adapting
Careers

When You Need
A New Job

174 Adapt or Perish

23

Knowledge of the Effects of Job Loss

By Emily Woodman-Nance

The Great Recession spanned from December 2007 to June 2009. According to the Bureau of Labor Statistics, "14.8 million people have lost their jobs since the start of the recession in December 2007."

The Miami Herald reports, "The government now estimates 8.4 million jobs vanished in the Great Recession. Economists also warn it will take until the middle of the decade for the job market to return to normal."

The media's response to this news is to have experts speak on topics such as *"How to Land a Job"* or *"How to Recession Proof Your Career"* or *"How to Prepare for a Job Fair or Interview."*

What about the emotional and mental effects job loss has on a person? Did you know that job loss is a major event equivalent to the loss of a loved one? Why is there little discussion or acknowledgement of the effects this devastating event has on people? A quick canvass of the media makes it clear that there is little interest in discussing this important topic. When have you seen, heard or read about the effects of job loss? I recently searched online for *"How to Land a Job"* and came up with 585,000,000 hits. I then searched *"How to Deal with Job Loss"* and *"How to Cope with Job Loss"* and came up with approximately 1,475,000 hits. What a discouraging difference!

Perhaps the effect of losing a job is not covered because the topic will not grab enough viewers, listeners or readers. Perhaps it is simply our nature as humans to provide solutions and band-aid other issues.

Coming from the perspective of a 20-year career as an Information Technology professional, I have seen that done. A band-aid solution was implemented either because of time and/or budget constraints. The underlying issue remained unaddressed. Of course, the issue eventually had to be addressed and as time passed, the adverse effect of the issue increased.

It works the same way with job loss. If not properly addressed, job loss can have a widespread impact that can grow later. In this chapter, I will discuss the effects of job loss and provide ways to cope with it. If you are employed, you will discover ways that you can assist your former co-workers, friends and/or loved ones.

If you have lost your job, what you are experiencing is normal. Loss of a job can trigger depression, anxiety and stress. For many it means the inability to pay bills, to get out of bed, and other problems.

It also hits self-esteem, raises doubt about your abilities, and creates a pessimistic outlook for the future. A sense of emptiness resembles grief, the same reaction that results from the loss of a loved one. Grief is very personal and is expressed in many ways. Most psychologists agree that there is a cycle of grief that people go through. The five stages of grief are:

- Denial
- Anger
- Bargaining
- Depression
- Acceptance

Although there is no quick answer to dealing with grief, it helps to express the feelings that come up. It is important to remember what you did in the past when you suffered a significant loss, find good listeners, and know your feelings are normal.

I personally know the effects of job loss. I was an Information Technology Consultant. In a consulting engagement, either the client or the consultant can end the engagement at will. As a consultant for close to two decades, I understood these rules of engagement. However, a client had never ended one of my consulting engagements at will until a certain contract with a Fortune 500 company abruptly terminated my contract that spanned about 18 months.

During that contract, I worked on two projects.

In the middle of the first project, I gave birth to a child. In an unprecedented move, the client put the project I was managing on hold while I was on maternity leave. I thought I was better than apple pie. The words that came up were, "You are the WOMAN!" Once I returned from leave, I resumed the project and my team completed it within the agreed upon time and budget. The project implementation was seamless and there was a great celebration.

I am still thinking, "You are the WOMAN!" I move on to another project. However, I do see that work is slowing down and people are being let go. In my head, I still believe I am golden. Then one summer morning around 11:45 a.m., I hear the following words from a voice message, *"Can you please call Joe?"* So, I call Joe. Joe says, *"It has nothing to do with your performance."* I immediately think, *"Wow, this is what he has probably been saying to others."* Joe went on to say, *"You can leave now or at the end of the day."* I think, *"This is so abrupt."* I let Joe know that I preferred to leave at the end of the day. After consuming a box of Kleenex, I composed myself well enough to leave the premises. Then the cycle of grief began.

Denial

I convinced myself that they did not really let me go. Technically the work they initially brought me on to manage had been completed months before. Therefore it was time for me to move on and do something different.

Anger

In a matter of days, I was angry. I thought and at times said, "The audacity of them letting me go. Don't they know I am the WOMAN!"

Bargaining

I bypassed this stage. I knew there was nothing I could do to reverse the decision. There was simply no additional work available.

Depression

Then sadness seeped in with a vengeance. A piece of my identity was gone. Unbeknownst to me, I had taken a hit to my self-esteem. I doubted my ability and emotional despair surfaced.

All this became clear when I went for an interview approximately two weeks after being let go. The location of the interview was five minutes from home. After one hour of driving around in circles, I called my best friend Lori. During our conversation, I realized it was way too soon for me to interview, let alone start back to work. I needed time to heal emotionally and mentally and come to grips with the abrupt ending of the consulting arrangement.

You may wonder what happened to the job interview. Despite my deep revelation, I showed up late for the interview. I was interviewed and extended an offer of employment. I did not accept for two reasons: (1) I was not ready to go back to work and (2) I did not want to work for a place that would think it is acceptable for a person to show up one hour late for an interview.

Acceptance

After several months, I finally accepted that I was let go and that was OK. I moved on to another consulting assignment.

Talking to my best friend definitely helped me work through the last stages of grief. If I had reached out to her sooner, I might have moved through the stages of grief more quickly.

According to Dr. Elisabeth Kubler-Ross, these stages do not necessarily come in the order noted above, nor are all stages experienced by everyone, though she stated a person will always experience at least two.

How you can help people who have lost their job?

First, think about what you would do if the person had lost a loved one. Now act. More than anything the person needs your support. The support can look like this:

- Going out for coffee
- Asking, "How can I support you?"
- Exercising together
- Reminding the person that this is a temporary setback

The key is to continue to see the person and not feel like you need to have all the answers. According to Michaela Pereira, co-anchor of the *KTLA Morning Show*, when she was unemployed she felt like she had some type of plague. Fortunately one person came around and took her out for coffee. To this day that person holds a special place in her heart.

[1] Bureau of Labor Statistics
[2] Miami Herald – Business section February 6, 2010

180 Adapt or Perish

24

Dealing with Job Loss and the Social Support System

By VaNessa Vollmer, Psy.D.

When people lose their jobs, it sometimes seems like sailing across the ocean with no idea what might come next.

Some days are perfect with a light breeze and gentle seas, warm sunshine and seagulls flying, pelicans gliding, and dolphins swimming. On other days your transition may feel like the perfect storm with impossible waves and high winds. You may wonder if all the skills, experience and lessons your mentors shared with you will be enough to weather the storm. You will need many different skills to best navigate this challenging time as an individual, a couple, a family and with your social support system.

You will experience the five stages of grief outlined by Dr. Kubler-Ross, **Denial, Anger, Bargaining, Depression** and eventual **Acceptance** of the situation. These stages of loss can come in any order until you reach Acceptance. **Denial** is when it's hard to believe that it's happening to you. **Anger** is when you find yourself with intense feelings toward whatever you think caused the situation. **Bargaining** begins when you wonder, "What if I would have just done… differently?" "What could I have done differently?"

Depression is the next stage. You realize you miss the people you used to work with, the potlucks, the camaraderie, telling jokes with former co-workers, and sharing experiences at work and in your personal life.

It's okay to feel sad and at the same time acknowledge that you had plenty of enjoyable times. These memories and the need to have fun and enjoy life don't go away when the job does.

Everyone has a unique length of time they think is normal to grieve the loss of a person or a job. People often read the book *How to Survive the Loss of a Love* and think it was written just for them. It was!

During this stage some may have thoughts of suicide and apathy and need professional assistance. Statistics show that the highest suicide rates occur in middle-aged, Caucasian males. It is important to give them social support during this time.

Eventually the desire to make new memories and plan new trips will become more attractive again. The five stages continue to bounce from stage to stage until you ask, "What can I learn from this?" and reach the Acceptance stage.

Acceptance is when you accept the situation, understand that it is temporary, learn something from it to make your life better in the future and apply it to making your life better. Set new goals, reflect on what worked before, improve on those skills and implement.

Your life goes on. You must resist the urge to withdraw and become a non-social, penny-pinching recluse. When people get depressed, they normally withdraw from friends, social activities, and entertaining. Happiness is replaced with irritability and inability to feel pleasure and enjoyment. If you feel down, recognize it first. Then listen to positive audio books online, in your car, or as you exercise.

Everyone understands about how long is normal to mourn a loss. Close relationships and friends will have similar patterns. When there is a difference between actual and expected times, social issues can develop.

For example, if it takes you a year or two to mourn a loss and others in your social group take six months, you may feel stress. Your normal timeline arises from your learned patterns from parents and others in your life or changes based on brain chemistry. When the depressing situation goes beyond a normal timeframe, some people may need to seek a medical assessment. It is important to recognize when you need help.

As you socialize and focus on getting better, you have options. It can be helpful to talk with someone who understands your situation and to develop your trusted personal board of directors.

Keep track of your hours, the contacts you make, and the number of applications and leads you follow up with. This is critical because whenever you feel like a frustrated, rejected victim, you will get a sense of empowerment from taking action on tasks you can control.

Remember that while you may not be able to control a hiring manager's decision to interview or hire you, you can control **what you think**, **how you feel** and **your own behavior**.

When you control these three things, you are doing the best you can to manage your new personal job duties: finding a job, changing careers, or learning about entrepreneurial endeavors through joining with like minded people to create a business.

Consider becoming an artist, which Seth Godin defines as "someone who brings humanity to a problem, who changes someone else for the better, who does work that can't be written down in a manual. Art is not about oil painting, it's about bringing creativity and insight to work instead of choosing to be just a compliant cog."

Remember, there are several options. If you decide to pursue a dream that you want to come true, seek guidance from mentors, make a plan, set aside funds to invest in your endeavor, and work your plan. If you don't know how to write a business plan and budget, you will find plenty of resources to help you.

Individual Organization

First things first! If you invest ten minutes to plan your week, you'll be ahead. Get a calendar and organize your meetings, job search time, networking, accountability partner meetings, leads and letters. If you have an office at home, make it your new work office, do a spring cleaning, and invest in your organization and planning.

Since you are managing your job search, you can make it a part or a full time job or act like it's a hobby. Of course, if you opt for the latter, you may get hobby results. It's okay to use this time to decompress from your previous job. However, as you rest read books, either audio, online, or printed, to keep up your professional development.

As you organize your office, first get business cards. Present yourself to your new company in a professional manner. Your cards will market you and distribute your contact information.

Personal branding is critical. You need to know what you do better than anyone else. Be able to explain it in 30 seconds or less. One friend who worked in marketing for years used to tell me, "If someone can't explain to me what they do or what their product does in 30 seconds, then I'm not sure they know and it wastes my time."

Manage your time like a business day. During daytime hours you can meet with or call people who are working, looking to hire, or networking. Locate professional organizations in your area and network there.

When I was coaching a military officer coming out of the service after 20 years, I recommended that he do this. Afterward, he called to say that this was one of the best, encounters he'd had with civilians in a long time. He made new professional business contacts and said that it felt strange since it was his first meeting where he was the **only** Marine in the room.

Since then he has made many professional contacts in corporate America, followed up with conversations, and connected with them on Linked-In to start his professional network.

Some people may feel uncomfortable with this process if they never had to look for work or had recruiters call them. They need to understand that this new skill is important for finding job leads, business opportunities, and connecting with more people who can introduce you to people they know.

The people in your network become your marketing department and make more people aware of your job search. They remember you and what you're looking for. When they hear of opportunities, they will share them with you.

The retired military officer went to networking meetings and met people who were hiring and people who could make professional introductions for him, thus creating an effective marketing plan he used to contact specific companies he was interested in working with. As a result, he landed a job in his area of interest, with similar corporate values, and in his desired geographic location.

Networking: Mindset and Social Skills Align

Going to networking meetings can be scary at first. If you go without getting the right mindset it's a challenge to get to the meeting. If you find networking difficult or uncomfortable, it's a challenge. I had a former colleague tell me, "VaNessa, you have this thing wired and network very well. However I could never do that myself because I'm shy and feel uncomfortable in those types of situations." She was partially correct and I commend her for having that insight. However, she may not have known why she felt uncomfortable.

Although your mom probably taught you to never talk to strangers, this exact social skill is required for doing successful business.

When you go to an event with a different mindset, it will work out differently for you. Most people go as a guest, a different mindset than that of a host/hostess. If you go to a networking event as a guest, you may assume a more passive role and wait for people to approach you. Attending an event with the mindset of a host/hostess is different. If you're the host you will feel more comfortable if you offer beverages to people or show them where the food is located. It is empowering because it is about helping others, not about being helped.

Introduce people to each other and watch the conversations take off. People need an icebreaker to get going and you can break the ice for them.

When you embrace the host/hostess mindset, you will navigate networking events more successfully and gain more information and contacts.

Get Organized to Network

Become familiar with online job search Boards, search engines and spider searches (which go to job boards and send you opportunities by email). These exist for levels of expertise from executive through management, individual contributor, technical, to administrative.

Write a professional resume or have someone review and evaluate your resume. Look professional on paper and in person. Remember, you get only one opportunity to make a good first impression.

If you are successful, then look successful!

From the top of your head to the tips of your toes, manage your professional appearance.

- Be current in your hairstyle and if you color it, keep roots looking natural.
- If you wear glasses, select a contemporary style.
- Keep your smile and teeth healthy and pearly white.
- Related to your speech, be sure to keep your vernacular appropriate for the market. Maintain quality mannerisms with your voice and breathe when you speak. Consider joining Toastmasters to improve your professional presentation skills.
- Vary your clothing so you don't look like you have a networking uniform on when you go to meetings. Be creative and consider an image consultant, not your teenager. (There is nothing worse than having someone get the wrong kind of attention by dressing inappropriately for their age.) Know classics and trends in wardrobe and dress appropriately for your profession. Wear colors that you look good in and styles that flatter your physique.
- Your health is important. Go to the doctor, get a physical and work out. Compare your biological age to your chronological age. Many websites offer this and add ideas for improved health practices and lifestyles. Work out to look and feel good. The mindset matters because happy people get hired.
- No one will recommend you if they do not think you will make them look good. Look professional since this is the first step to getting that next opportunity.

Perception and appearance is reality. Practice being an authentic and respected resource for others. Build relationships to connect with others. It is a healthy practice and a sign of good social skills to genuinely mean it when you ask others how they are doing. Some people may not ask because it might be uncomfortable for them to hear about your situation. That's their issue, not yours.

Continue your sense of service, compassion and leadership when you are in transition. This includes being a good role model for others.

Networking

One introduction can change your life. You never know who knows the person who wants to hire you or can put you in touch with a company looking for your skills and talents.

People do business with people for two reasons; they **like** them and they **trust** them.

Remember to be gracious and practice listening skills. Be interesting to them and stay engaged when you listen. Keep the conversation balanced. If you're talking, they aren't always listening. They may be thinking about what to say next. However if you talk about them and reflect information you just heard back to them, they will listen and let you know if your understanding is accurate. This is called reflective listening and is great for communication and building relationships.

Building your brand is important to creating awareness of the value you bring to others. If this is awkward, remember what you did to develop your organization or company brands. Apply those skills to help others understand what you do. Read books like *Branding from the Inside* and understand how to apply these skills. This will help you in your career and make you a better business person.

During the networking process, practice being a consultative sales person. Show yourself as the expert, get to know your client better and have a private agenda that needs to include:

1. Purpose for attending the meeting,
2. Specific goals to accomplish like meeting the speaker and panelists, or other key attendees,
3. Plans to follow up in a timely manner.

When attending an event, **sit with strangers** and talk with them so that you meet more people. Don't sit with people you already know. This way you can network with others, introduce friends to them, and meet new people who can you give professional introductions.

Prepare a list of questions to get the information that you want. Introduce others to each other even if you don't know both of them. There is always an opportunity for business synergy to take place.

Conscientiousness is important for job success and life success! What you say and how you make it meaningful for people is important. Many people are used to the "take and receive" process. However, if you ask first how you can help, you open the door and will usually get help in a reciprocal relationship.

Many very successful people become more than a resource, they figure out what they can do to help others. People I know have assisted with financial issues, health issues, or shared an article or the name of a doctor. This sincere effort to help shows that you care.

Internal strength of character is important during times of transition. I've heard the saying before that "crisis does not develop character, it reveals it." This is true on many levels. Transition is fertile soil where your current personal growth will be sown, grown and harvested several times over.

How Do You Manage Stress?

I have asked people, "What bothers you the most in life?" I usually get a thoughtful, reflective pause and many answers. I then ask them this question: "Have you ever been bitten by a lion?" Usually they respond, "No" so I ask, "Have you ever been bitten by a bear?" and they respond, "No." I ask then, "Have you ever been bitten by a shark?" and I hear "No." Then I ask them, "How many of you have been bitten by a mosquito?" I usually hear a unanimous "Yes!" then I ask, "How about a spider?" Again, I hear another "yes" and then "Ever been bitten by a flea or an ant?" Again, I hear another "yes" in unison. I then ask, "Isn't it more important to watch out for the big things in life because you can usually see them coming and can avoid them? Now we have proof that it's really the little things in life that can eat you up." Everyone nods their heads, agrees and says "Yes" then smiles at each other.

Some assessments measure the number of life events that you have experienced over the last 12 months and create a scale that tells you when stressful events will affect your physical health. It is the Holmes & Rahe Social Readjustment Rating Scale and is available online.

Other assessments tell you how well you manage stress. Some people may experience a high level of stress and handle it well while others may manage it poorly, even with lower stress levels. You can read many books to help you cope with stress on both a physical and mental level. Many people know how to get stressed and uptight. Very few people know how to relax.

You can address physical stress in many ways. For instance, include regular exercise like yoga to become more aware of your breathing and muscle tension. Always check with a doctor before beginning new physical activity for safety reasons. You can combine activities like riding a bike at the gym and listening to an audio book, or walking through a park and enjoying nature.

Massage is an option because the masseuse can relax tight muscles for you. You will still benefit from it even if you fall asleep. In moderation, a Jacuzzi helps improve circulation and relax and tone muscles.

Social support systems are important because people need healthy ways to cope with challenging times that will eventually pass. No matter what the economy is doing, people need ways to feel good and make progress. Some may select healthier ways to feel better than others. Embrace your loved ones and friends during this time and be supportive because everyone can more easily receive a part of your heart than a piece of your mind.

Moderation is the key to balance. While some prefer escapism like excessive reading or going to movies, others may exercise or clean and others will self-medicate. Poverty and social isolation are associated with increased risk of psychiatric problems in general. Nearly 17.6 million adults in the US are alcoholics or have alcohol problems. Others may prefer other substances.

The marijuana of the 60's and 70's is not the same as that grown hydroponically now. New marijuana has 20% higher THC levels and can cause withdrawal symptoms. The psychological effects of marijuana include: distorted sense of time, paranoia, magical thinking, short-term memory loss, anxiety, and depression.

Abusing marijuana can result in problems with memory, learning, and social behavior. It can interfere with family, school, and work. Suicide occurs almost twice as often as murder in marijuana users. Each year about 32,000 people in the US commit suicide. About 45% of the homeless have serious substance abuse problems, 23% have a mental illness and 8% are infected with HIV or AIDS.

When you learn how to deal with stress in ways that make you feel more in control, you improve your health, your relationships and your work. Each year drug abuse results in around 40 million serious illnesses or injuries among people in the US. Melancholic depression is a type of depression whose symptoms include an inability to feel pleasure, physical agitation, insomnia, and decreased appetite. If you feel depressed and it goes on for a time, contact a doctor or therapist to see if you need further social support.

Develop a strategy to get help from others because you're better off when you don't do it alone. As Wayne Dyer reminds us, "Sometimes we are spiritual beings having a human experience." Stay positive, have resources to read or listen to when the white knuckle rollercoaster goes up with interviews and down when things don't go the way you want.

Keep your options open to learning what you can do better by being authentic and being a great resource for others. Have friends to call when you need to vent. Let them know that you need to vent before you release all the stuff built up from your challenges.

If you have a Smart phone, buy apps with Stress Quotes, Success Quotes and other inspirational words to get you back on track. Listen to audio books on inspirational topics when you're feeling low and need to get refocused.

Take moments, hours and days one at a time. Recognize the distress cycle and get back on the success cycle with the help of friends, family and fellow colleagues.

There is always a way to do it better...find it. – Thomas Edison

Resources
Dyer, Wayne (2005) *The Power of Intention*
Kubler Ross, Elisabeth (1969). *On Death and Dying*
Pink, Daniel (2007). *The Dip: A Little Book That Teaches You When to Quit (and When to Stick)*

25

Preparing for Job Change

By Mark Fierle

Many years ago I learned that markets go up and down over time, from the tight money of the late 60s, when even highly paid executives couldn't buy a home, to the late 70s when inflation created interest rates on home mortgages in excess of 21%, to the late 80s S&L bust. The late 90s had its Dot-com debacle and now look where we are.

When we are in a down period there are lots of opportunities! What I've also figured out is when we are in an up time we think it will never end and when we are in a down period we think it will never end. But they always do. Our world is never static. Sounds like a paradigm shift.

Let's look at where came from and where we are now. When we think back over the past 150 years, from the Second Industrial Revolution forward, we find that most of the great inventions in both medicine and industry came about during down times. Ask why and we will see that it was because someone found a need and endeavored to fill it. This is marketing 101 and like the theme of this book and like Darwin's survival of the fittest, either Adapt or Perish! When we are knocked out of our rut, a state of urgency sets in (some say the greatest motivator) and we find a way to get that career or job we always wanted or move to the place we always wanted to live. With security no longer a reason not to move or change careers as in the past, now is the time to talk to that head hunter that has been calling you for years or take those classes you have been putting off that will enable you to get to the next level. As with the greatest inventions, many people are choosing to follow their dreams by changing careers during the "down times." An example may be when the real estate boom went bust, many smart people bought franchises in an area they loved and re-energized both their career and their income. Jobs, like almost everything else, have life spans. Take advantage of those opportunities and follow your dreams.

When I talk to young candidates about careers, I relate the perfect career to the perfect marriage. While I have been happily married to the same woman for many years, I always say there was only one perfect marriage. That was Adam and Eve. You see Adam didn't have to hear about all the guys Eve could have married and Eve didn't have to hear about Adam's mothers cooking! That's the way it goes with careers. There are few perfect careers so don't be afraid to try something new, especially if it's something you always thought would be interesting. The excuse to not do this should never be: "I've never done that or I didn't get my degree in that field." A good friend in human resources used to tell me that he encouraged his employees to annually seek out an interview in another company or in another field. When I first heard him say this at a meeting of HR Execs eyebrows went up↑. Then he explained that frequently after people have been at a company for a while they begin to take things for granted and often think the grass is greener someplace else. Sometimes it is and sometimes it isn't. The only way to find out is check it out. You may find it's not so bad where you are. On the other hand, this exercise may prompt you to take action.

Here are a few examples of action:

- Learn to adapt and get comfortable with change. We are all somewhat different than we were ten years ago and believe me we will be different ten years from now. So let's get comfortable with today and tomorrow. Maybe we can even learn something new. By the way, do you tweet?
- Make a complete list of your skills and add an adjective that describes your competence in that area. Example: knowledgeable, expert, familiar with etc. Then make a second

list of the things you have done over the course of your career that you are most proud of. Just start thinking and writing without quantifying. You can do that later. Suggestion: start most recently and go backward. This will prompt your memory and you will think of things that perhaps you haven't thought of in years. When you are done, "quantify" by noting how they made money, saved money or saved time. You can then think of the story of how you came up with that conclusion. These lists are to help us when we are feeling low. We can look at them and realize: "I'm not so bad after all! Actually I'm pretty good and they are lucky to have me!"

This can even be helpful when interviewing and you are asked, "Why should I hire you?" Instead of giving some subjective answer like, "I work hard, eat my lunch at my desk and never take time off to go to the dentist, etc.," give a results-oriented answer like while at XWZ Co. I was able to create a system that made money, saved money or saved time for the organization. Then ask, "How can I help you?" When they start asking questions like, "How did you do that?" it means they are interested! It also creates a dialogue not a monologue, a good thing I might add. It pays to learn to speak comfortably about yourself and the things you have done. It also makes you as a problem solver and helps brand and differentiate you from others.

Here are some other suggestions:

- **Learn to speak and write like an expert.** When you are looking for work or thinking of changing professions, these are two skills that companies and organizations are thirsting for. They both help get your and their message out. Take some writing classes, work at getting something published and become involved in Toastmasters.
- **Become an expert on something of value.** Whether or not it is a new or old technology, you will be surprised who calls you for advice on the subject, asks you to make a presentation to a large group or even to the Board of Directors. They may even pay you money for your knowledge. As you know money is almost as good as cash! (thanks Yogi)
- **Learn to be customer service oriented.** That is, give more and expect more. Step up your volunteer work. You will be

surprised who you will meet at charitable endeavors. It also looks good on your resume.

26

Financial Adaptation and stress: What's Your Burn Rate?

By VaNessa Vollmer, Psy.D.

Your boss has just handed you your last check. What do you do? First, you need to tell your significant other, "I no longer have a job." The first conversation you have with your spouse includes urgent questions like,

- How much money do we have?
- Do we need me to go to work?
- Do we need to lease out our home and rent? Or Sell?
- What about our medical insurance?
- What are we going to do for food?
- What about the kids and school?

What items do you burn through while in transition?

Budgeting, finances, relationships and health instantly come to mind. Setting priorities is preparation to adapt financially!

Individuals wonder, "What is a healthy financial burn rate while transitioning between jobs?" People can do several key things to adapt during this time. Some may feel overwhelmed and others may avoid or ignore the problem. The payoff comes from information collection, making the best proactive decisions and planning your results.

Burning through assets like time, energy, and money affects health and relationships.

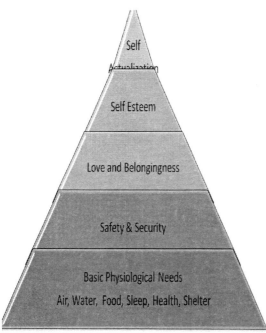

We are all familiar with various pyramids used to show priorities that build on lower levels to advance to higher levels. Two of the more common are the Food Pyramid used by nutritionists and Abraham Maslow's Hierarchy of Needs in classic psychology. The Financial Pyramid is based closely on the Maslowian approach to human actualization in that basic needs must be met first before a person advances to higher levels of existence. A person unable to provide basic nutrition for themselves will find it difficult to have any concern for their safety, to advance to higher levels of relationships, or achieve their dreams. In financial strategy the same is true. Preparing for catastrophic events and paying off credit cards should come before investing in high risk stocks or futures.

When people get their priorities reversed, high risk increases and the consequences can be drastic.

Maslow's Hierarchy of Needs is a visual model that addresses the various levels of needs. We all have the same needs, no matter which level we are at on the hierarchy.

When in transition it is important to keep priorities and basic needs aligned with your resources.

Build from the Bottom up

- Maintain **basic physiological needs** like water, food, sleep, and shelter. These are musts when making decisions affecting your future plan to adapt during transition. During economically challenging times, it is critical to lay a strong foundation for achieving progressive levels of needs and success.
- Many adaptations in the community occur when faith-based organizations reach out to those in need with food programs and community-based health or shelter programs.
- If you go through a foreclosure, short sale, or other major life change, you realize shelter is usually the largest budget item and a critical need to meet. Most people need some shelter and an address to find and maintain employment. It's one of the first items you complete on a job application.
- Many families adapt to shelter needs as multiple generations of families live under one roof. Smaller families or singles rent smaller places or rooms. This conserves funds and resources and supports several levels of the hierarchy of needs, sometimes at the cost of previous privacy. If you have these options to meet your temporary shelter needs, this allows you to progress to the next level of needs: safety and security.

Safety and Security

- Safety and security levels address your body, resources, family, property, employment, and maintaining good physical health. You can have all the money in the world but if you don't have your health, what good is it?
- Keep your personal and financial priorities aligned and build the foundations of meeting your needs for the best results.
- Financially this is the burn stage. You have employment with an income stream that meets safety and security needs; however you may not have enough for extras like networking events and investment in professional development.

Belongingness and Love

Friendship, family, professional and networking relationships are the next level of needs.

When you hear that a colleague in transition is unable to attend a meeting because they can't afford it, suggest that they volunteer for the meeting rather than paying full price. That way they still get the same benefit: Learn from the presentation and network.

At this financial burn stage, you may want to invest in a few, select business networking events.

Self Esteem Needs

At this level, confidence, self-esteem, achievement, respect for others, and respect by others are needs to be met. Advanced learning takes place at this level because supportive needs are already met.

Self Actualization

Vitality, creativity, self sufficiency, authenticity, playfulness, and meaningfulness are among the needs at this level.

When your brain can focus on higher ordered functions such as creativity, authenticity and meaningfulness, you experience synergy because you are "reaping the rewards" of your work on many professional levels. This happens when you're at your personal, spiritual and professional peak.

Financial Pyramid Needs

The basic levels on the financial pyramid of needs include tools to support your search: transportation, networking events, professional resumes, and business cards to exchange with other professionals. Collect income tax data like mileage records, schedules and meeting locations, with whom you met, and the related receipts for breakfasts, lunches, dinners, coffee, and parking receipts. You can collect information the old fashioned way or leverage newer tools that make your life easier.

If you're going to use the old fashioned way, place your receipts in an envelope for the year. Newer technical tools include streamlined systems to collect data.

You can take these portable technical tools on trips:
- To register expenses use Neat Receipts.

- For mileage use apps. They track mileage for business, personal and charity work with respective reimbursement rates. Download this information into Excel spreadsheets, keep one and give one to your tax professional.

Phone communication and laptops are essential for working in this age of information. If you don't have your resume or profile up on LinkedIn, learn the site's basic and advanced features.

- Basic information: Input your name, company names, job titles, education and interests into your profile with your contact information. This helps recruiters find you when you are in transition.
- Advanced information: Post examples of your professional work such as PowerPoint presentations, blog posts, and professional books you've read. LinkedIn allows you to upload your resume, professional picture and customized preferences.

You can also participate with interactive group discussions. Select professional groups to include in your profile. Subscribe to group discussions with daily or weekly email delivery. Answer questions other members ask and share those answers with your professional network. Professional belongingness needs are met at this level to support business interactions.

This way you meet and build relationships with professionals with similar interests and values.

Groups and companies also post related job opportunities. In addition, you can follow LinkedIn and other social platforms to allow you to electronically select companies or recruiters and to be notified immediately when jobs are posted. The basic service is free to most users. Recruiters pay to access and search for candidates. LinkedIn and other social networks are platforms where you share your credentials and expertise for professionals who need your talent.

Become more familiar with social media and how to leverage it for your search. There are several ways to input job search criteria into sites like www.Indeed.com, www.SimplyHired.com and others that will go out to other websites, collect information, and deliver job leads via e-mail. Useful websites like these can help you streamline your job search process.

Selected websites have job search apps for Smart phones. Literally, these are job opportunities at your fingertips! If you carry a dumb phone, this is a missed opportunity.

Professional Branding Burn Rate

Professionals can utilize different methods and information platforms to become well branded. How do you do this? Ask yourself, "What is it that you do better than anyone else?" Offer information about your strengths and personal brand on various media which are available free or for a nominal fee depending on your marketing budget and acceptable burn rate:

- Blogs- Wordpress
- Twitter (microblog)
- Facebook - Networking
- Linked-In - Networking
- Ning – your own social network
- You Tube – Video

Thoroughly research the current tools available for job search opportunities. Include your personal brand statement that distinguishes what makes you special professionally. You need to include this tag line in all media, whether you're looking for full time opportunities, contract work, or building your own new business. What your personal brand statement says about you is key information for people who need your services or expertise to help their company succeed. Invest time to research this topic online and think about it carefully.

Why is branding so important? Companies invest in branding. Think carefully about what goes into your brand because it needs to clearly identify your professional strengths, solutions, and value to an employer.

My friend, Stu in Marketing, shared a tip, "If you can't tell me what you or your product does in 30 seconds or less, I get bored." Be brief and focused.

Remember, your personal brand is your tag line. Make it brief, practical and memorable.

You can check other websites for new ways to organize your information in free and open source software like www.lifehack.org. If you need something, search the web to see if it exists first. Technology is a fertile ground for planting ideas based on ever changing business needs. When they say that, "Necessity is the mother of invention," it's especially true of technology.

Financial Burn Rate and Social Needs

Financial matters are a challenge when it comes to socializing during this time and yes, socializing is a necessity. Humans are social creatures and need healthy interaction.

Instead of going to the more expensive places, you could eat when working or shift to less frequent dining. There is a natural tendency to socially withdraw that you need to recognize. Make a conscious decision to find a creative way to work dining with others into your social calendar.

You won't be expected to throw extravagant parties when you're in transition. However, since we are still social beings, you can participate in free or low cost activities like walking in a park or having a picnic. Potlucks work well since everyone brings a dish to share and socializes together without the sole financial burden being on one person.

Beneficial results are:
- Dispersed costs
- Decreased stress
- Maintains and supports healthy social interaction
- Normalizes needs being met during a challenging time
- Reframes your situation and facilitates a deeper understanding for significant other/spouse so they can see that you are in the company of other talented individuals.

Remember the childhood story of Stone Soup? The story is about a town hit hard by financially challenging times. A person placed a stone in a large pot of boiling water. When people noticed him they asked what he was doing. He explained that he was making a very tasty Stone soup. When people asked him what it tasted like, he asked members of the community to contribute a small edible ingredient and he would share the soup with them. Many did and as a result created a pot filled with delicious soup that all could enjoy. Share its lesson with your community. You'd be surprised at how many people respond generously when asked.

Adapting Finances and Relationships

I have heard an out-of-work executive say many times that his or her significant other doesn't understand the job search process. "Why don't you just go out and get a job?!?" they say. This conflict can lead to depression or in 59% of cases, divorce.

One way I helped people get past this misunderstanding was to help the spouses understand better. A colleague and I decided to host quarterly events for both job seekers and spouses to continue the socializing we normally do. This kept their spirits up and encouraged everyone to keep looking. This has been a huge success for years. At these events, people talked about new leads, new consulting opportunities, possible organizational restructuring, and related jobs. The experience and energy was healthy for everyone.

When spouses of those in transition attend and meet other people in transition, they realize that job loss affects many intelligent people. They are pleasantly surprised to see the level of quality talent. Some may even get ideas that they can utilize at their work. I call this a "reality check" because:

- They are reassured that they or their spouses are not alone in this time of change, even though it may feel that way.
- That other unemployed people look just like everyone else!

During times of high unemployment people need to realize that unemployment is not the fault of the unemployed but results from more people wanting to work than there are available jobs.

These events are safe, fun and normalizing places where people enjoy themselves in a relaxed environment, share information, and network. Unemployed people who network and attend conferences sometimes share handouts or PowerPoint presentations with their unemployed friends so they can stay current since having a job takes priority. If you're working on an important project, you don't always have time to attend other professional events. Everyone has fun and everyone builds relationships that lead to professional connections, possibly becoming co-workers, and even long term friendships.

Adapting Through Financial Advisors

When you're in transition, meet with your professional financial advisor(s) for a financial check up.

This professional will help you assess where you are and create a plan to decrease your financial and resource burn rate. Develop several alternative plans to deal with contingencies. Consider the worst possibilities so you can consider options before they happen.

Unemployment benefits last only so long. Use your funds wisely during lean times to stay financially healthy longer.

If you don't have a budget, develop one now. Several executives have leased their homes and moved into apartments to save money. If the numbers work, this is an option.

If the numbers still don't work, seriously consider selling to adapt. High numbers of short sales and foreclosures in both investment property and primary residences have plagued the real estate market recently because of job loss and decisions to rebalance personal budgets.

I facilitated groups for several years for the District Attorney's Office for people who needed to change their beliefs about and behavior with money. After this group learning opportunity, they could recognize early warning signs, high risk situations, and steps they could take to prevent future problems. Since we don't teach personal budgeting in school and since they hadn't learned it later, I worked with them to create a budget that made sense.

Budget Guidelines and Ideas

In a budget, weigh your needs and wants against resources. Too many people have no idea where their finances stand.

First, create an "estimated" budget and compare it to your "actual" budget to get a realistic picture of what is coming in and going out.

Budget Guideline Percentages Based on Your Income:
- Monthly housing payment not more than 25 to 33%.
- Car and insurance payment: about 7 to 10%.
- Credit Card payments no more than 5% of your income.
- Save a minimum of 10%.

Fill in all of your other expenses such as food, clothing, utilities, entertainment, medical and healthcare, repairs and maintenance, charity/donations, vacations, holidays, investments and emergency fund. Calculate what percentages these are in your budget.

To record the actual budget numbers, keep a log of income and every purchase you make, bills paid, and money saved for one month minimum. Keep a log with you and include impulse purchases like gum, mints, or fast food, so you can see where money slips through your fingers.

Second, be certain that more money is coming in than going out. Compare your "estimated" and "actual" budgets for your financial "reality check."

If more money is going out, then rebalance your budget. If necessary, use coupons and get a part time job. Remember "some peanuts are better than no peanuts."

If you need ideas for saving money consider online resources like www.eHow.com or books on the finances. Your cost of living is a large piece of the pie for implementing sustainable, successful budgets.

Educate yourself so you can make informed decisions. Ask friends how they save money. Ask your financial advisor for additional tips on budgets, investments, and protecting your resources during this transition time.

Transition Networking, Coffee and Lunch Meetings

Most people pay their own way while in transition or take turns buying each other lunch or coffee. At times someone out of work less time may offer to buy lunch for the person who has been out longer. Other times it's reciprocated. If you ask someone for their expertise, tell them, "I'd like to pick your brain and I'll buy you lunch." This doesn't mean that you invite someone to lunch and then later they send you a bill. If you're going out with an expert or colleague clarify in advance what the payment arrangements are and what is to be discussed. Bartering is an option.

A meal out every now and then is fine although I've notice many more people eating at home and growing gardens again. Farmers Markets often carry fresh produce at a better price than in the grocery store.

People who are working also give gift cards to unemployed people. The key to healthy perspectives during transition is balance. Ask yourself what your financial priorities are. Again, keep a healthy balance. Some people cut back so severely that they get depressed. Keep things in moderation and enjoy a special treat now and then.

Transition is a great time to reflect on what money means to you and become more aware of your beliefs about money.

Some people use money as a tool, it comes, it goes, and it comes again. Others use money to cope with a down day by going shopping or seeing a movie to get a temporary good feeling. Some people do this over and over again without knowing why.

Financial Awareness

Metacognition is a fancy word that means having the "ability to be aware of what, why, and how we think" about behavior, thoughts, feelings and our interactions with our environment. This includes financial awareness and our relationship with money.

This time of transition is best leveraged for personal awareness, development and growth. Understanding ourselves gives us a better insight into why we are the way we are, and how we want to adapt for the future. We can then find tools, knowledge, and mentors that facilitate our transformation.

Since each personal situation is unique, you need to decide on the best options for your family for health insurance, investments, food, essentials, entertainment, socializing, job and career search, professional development and more. Consider making a list of the items most important to you and prioritize them as part of your personal financial planning.

Read or re-read books on money like the *Millionaire Next Door* and *Think and Grow Rich* and others to educate yourself about your options. Susie Orman has written some great books that deal with beliefs about money.

Bottom line, if you haven't had the opportunity before, invest now in gaining more knowledge so you can maximize your personal and business resources to adapt for long term financial success.

Remember, your personal economy has two elements: things you do and things you promise to do. Both rely on belief (credit) and some degree of predictability (with it most credit will be honored most of the time). If performance gets seriously out of line with promises then chaos results: nobody knows what is happening, everyone loses belief (credit), and the system becomes at risk of burning out of control.

206 Adapt or Perish

This relates to a question that my Dad used to ask me when I was young, "Would you prefer to have dollars or cents?" I thought dollars are more money than cents." So, I picked "Dollars, Daddy" to which my Dad would reply, Dollars only take you so far, however if you have 'sense' you can make all the dollars you need. I got the answer wrong, until I figured out that it sounded like cents, but he really meant "sense." Before we can spell, we can still learn the value of sense versus a dollar.

Get educated, brush up on the basics and take the control back. Collect your information, know what your burn rate is and make informed decisions. Like a skilled pilot navigating turbulence, it's a temporary bumpy ride. Knowing your financial burn rate and options is reassuring while you're in a temporary "holding pattern" until you safely land your next opportunity.

Resources:

Hill, Napolean (revised 2011). *Think and Grow Rich: Original 1937*
Orman, Suze (2006). *The 9 Steps to Financial Freedom: Practical and Spiritual Steps so You can Stop Worrying*
Orman, Suze (2006). *Suze Orman's Guidebook: Put The 9 Steps to Work*
Orman, Suzie (2008). *Suze Orman's 2009 Action Plan: Keeping Your Money Safe and Sound*
Stanley, Thomas and Danko, William. (2010).*The Millionaire Next Door: The Surprising Secrets of America's Wealthy*

27

Making a Great First Impression

By Steve Amos

Job interviewing is not our specialty. Doing our job is our specialty. Most of us go years between interviews and are horribly out of practice when the time comes. Here are some tips to get you ready.

Prepare! Prepare! Prepare!

Was that a clear warning? The worst mistake you can make in an interview is winging it. Great salespeople prepare for every meeting. You also need to prepare.

First get to know yourself as a valued employee. Take time to think about your accomplishments at every job you have had. Take lots of notes. If you dig deep enough, you will find major accomplishments every one to two years. If you have any awards, success memos or company literature, dig it out. Go through your records to remind yourself of other successes.

Add to this list volunteer work where you have accomplishments. How about during school? Sports teams? This is important. Spend time finding out how good you are. It will help you market and sell yourself for that next job.

Talking about accomplishments differentiates you from other job hunters who talk only about responsibilities. If you did it for the last company, you can do it here is the message.

Power Stories

My friend John Hall teaches his students to tell Power Stories about themselves. To create such a story, ask yourself these questions and write down the answers:

What was the problem or situation?

What specifically did you contribute to the solution? We all work in teams, but your contribution helps accomplish the mission. Write down the actions you took.

What were the results? You need to quantify these results. Do you know the dollars, the quantities, the percentages or the time that was earned or saved? If you don't know, give your best estimates. The military calls this "taking a SWAG," which is a "scientific wild assed guess." Seriously, just put together how many per day, how many hours per day, what were people paid per hour (including benefits) and estimate the value as honestly as possible. I teach people not to exaggerate because you never know who you will interview with. One student we had interviewed with her old boss and asked what he thought of the numbers. He replied, "That was about right," which is what you want to hear.

Now write the story about the accomplishment and practice telling it out loud until it feels natural. I have a Word document with the bullet points and the stories written out. When I review it before the interview, I am ready with examples for the questions asked.

How many responsibilities can you turn into accomplishments?

Dress Up

I know most companies are okay with casual dress. Suits and ties are disappearing from the workplace where I live. But that is after you get the job. The standards for interviewing are still stricter than when you work there.

Dr. Vanessa Vollmer tells how she had a first interview and wore a suit as she usually does and met with executive level people. It went well that day, however it was mentioned to her that they don't wear suits at the office where she would be interviewing next. One of the people she knew in the process advised her to go to the next interview dressed business casual. The next follow-up interview was on a Friday. Her friends encouraged her to dress business casual so that she'd fit in better. But the second interview did not go well. She was appropriately and conservatively dressed for an employee, but she was not yet on the team. In short, that may have contributed to her not getting that job. An important lesson learned: Don't dress like an employee until you are one.

Have at least one very good business suit for interviewing, including a couple of shirts and ties. If you have not worn a suit in a while, put one on and go to church or events. You have to rehearse so on the day of the interview the suit feels natural. It also takes longer to dress than normal, so you need to rehearse to prevent being late for the interview.

If I go back for a second interview, I wear the same suit. It makes the interviewers comfortable that you are the same person they talked to earlier. This is from research done by John Molloy, author of *Dress for Success*. This may not work for women, but a similar outfit with slightly different accessories or color blouse may work.

This may seem like over preparing, but why create distractions during an interview?

Know as Much as Reasonable about the Company

You also want to know what you can about who you are interviewing with. Search for the company with Google, Yahoo and Bing. What are they famous for? Is there any business news on Yahoo Finance? What new products or services do they offer? Can you read about all the divisions related to the company? Who are the competitors?

Do the same thing with the people you may interview with. Who are they and where did they come from? LinkedIn is a great resource. Do you have anything in common with them? Remember. It is not the company who makes the decision, but the people involved.

Tell Me about Yourself

This question will be first question in almost every interview. They don't want a life story; they want to know how you can help them get their work done. Have your answer prepared and rehearsed. You want to be able to tell it without it sounding canned. Keep your answer short.

Ask Good Questions

Always ask good questions about the position, responsibilities and the company culture. I like having 6 to 10 questions ready. The goal is to find out what they need.

- What do you feel are the key skills required to be successful in this position?
- Describe the three top challenges that I'll face in this job?
- What are the key deliverables that this position must achieve?
- What has to happen for you to know you've hired the best person?

Attitude

First impressions are very important. Believe it or not the first 10 to 20 seconds can make or break you. I have heard senior people say they knew the person was not really qualified, but they liked them so much they were trying to justify hiring them, or think of other openings they fit during the interview.

You want to be comfortable to work with, have good energy, and be on their wavelength if possible. You want to understand what they are asking you and answer the right question during your interview. You want to show your skills and talent in the best light.

I believe in eliminating distractions from my mind when I am interviewing. I go into the interview assuming I want the job. I assume I am going to get the job, and I act as if I already work there. I just haven't gotten a paycheck yet.

I do this so my mind is not thinking, "Do I really want to work here?" during the interview. I will have time to decide on the drive home, and I have turned down jobs after I went home. But thinking about that during the interview may distract me from paying attention to what they are saying and asking.

Assuming I will get the job sounds presumptuous. However, I don't know who I am competing with and can't control that. If they have a better match, I may be out no matter what I do. So I focus on doing my best selling and let the results happen. Besides, the next interview may be for an even better job.

Why do I act as if I already work there? Remember, the biggest question they have is not whether you are qualified. Their biggest question is whether they will like working with you 8 to 10 hours per day. Will you be a good employee and not cause trouble? I already have a good personality and work hard without supervision. Why not demonstrate that in the interview? This way they see what they will get and I get to be my natural self, which is less stressful. The interviewer and I get to see if we can work together. Do you see how this prevents you from acting nervous?

Thank You Letters

You may not get the job because of the letter, but you will put yourself back in front of them again. Keep the note short, sell any points you think best present you has a great candidate, and have a great attitude. This will make you stand out as someone who follows through.

Summary

Interviewing is part marketing, part sales and part art. The simplest way to look at it is that an interview is just a business conversation. As soon as I can, I get past the question and answer period and turn the interview into a business conversation. This is where the interviewer and I are more comfortable.

Turning the interview into a business conversation is a very good buy signal. You have earned the confidence of the person you are talking to and they are starting to see you working with them. Both are good for selection time.

Now get prepared. What accomplishments are you proud of?

212 Adapt or Perish

28

Adapt or Stagnate

By John Hall

*"Most men lead lives of quiet desperation
and go to the grave with the song still in them."*

This often quoted observation from Henry David Thoreau's *On Walden Pond* was made in 1840. Sometimes I wonder if this observation is as relevant in the 21st century as it was in the 19th century. Based on over 20 years of coaching individuals through career transitions, I have concluded that the majority of working men and women, from PhDs to dropouts, fail to reach their potential. They take potluck jobs hoping that their ideal position will be just around a corner that often fails to materialize. And so in some small way many are "living lives of quiet desperation."

Why do the majority of 21st century men and women plateau well below their potential? I believe it comes down to seven factors that often start in the teen years:

1. Having to choose a career with little life experience
2. Not knowing or considering core values and motivated skills
3. Poor transition planning
4. Settling for potluck jobs
5. Undervaluing the soft skills

6. Lack of strategic career planning
7. Lack of personal branding

Choosing a Career with Little Life Experience

For most middle-class men and women, work is the single most important thing in their lives. Yet one of the great paradoxes of human development is that we are required to make the most important decision of our life as pimple-faced adolescents or very young adults, before we have the knowledge, judgment and self-understanding to choose wisely. Yet the pressure to make a career choice is tremendous because entry into the 21st century work world is increasingly difficult due to the overwhelming increase in the number of occupations from which to choose and because the increasingly complex nature of most jobs has made training longer and more expensive.

Failure to Consider Core Values and Motivated Skills

"Who do you feel is the most successful individual, Donald Trump or Mother Teresa?"

This is a question I have asked clients and students perhaps a hundred times. Often it leads to enlightened discussions on personal values. Is money important to you or is helping others of greater importance? Both money and helping are only two of perhaps fifty values to consider when making career choices. Some others are:

Independence	Change and Variety
Creative Expression	Public Contact
Challenging Problems	Intellectual Status
Status	Time Freedom
Security	Moral Fulfillment
Stature	Work Life Balance

This list is only a fraction of the values you should consider when making a career choice. An excellent resource for identifying career values is the *Career Values Card Sort* by Dick Knowdell.

Lack of Strategic Career Planning

"Raise your hand if you have ever been involved with strategic planning for an organization?" Typically 80 percent of hands go up in audiences of managers and executives I have spoken to over the last two decades. I follow that question with, "How many of you have used the same strategic planning principles to plan your own career?" This question results in less than five percent raising hands.

In the world of downsizing, rightsizing, offshore manufacturing, with jobs going to India, China, and who knows where else, we all must adapt to the fact that we are entrepreneurs. In this environment long-term career success depends on strategic planning, which includes developing a high profile in your function and industry communities that brands you in your professional community.

Steven Covey, in his book *The 7 Habits of Highly Effective People*, stresses the importance of strategic planning for long-term career success. One element of a strategic plan is a Mission Statement, which Covey views as your North Star, helping to keep you moving toward your long-term goals even when the winds of life begin blowing your ship off course. Once completed, you should frame and display the mission statement where you will view it every day as a constant reminder of how you intend to impact your professional world.

A Mission Statement takes the Personal/Career Theme and puts it into words in a manner that defines your career's future direction and your efforts and activities in very broad terms. Keep it simple, crisp and to the point.

State your goal of becoming successful in your career field.

_____

_____

_____

Define a specific niche within your career field.

_____

_____

_____

_____

Define definite geographic boundaries.

_____

_____

_____

_____

State how you will achieve your mission.

_____

_____

_____

Example: *"To clearly establish and maintain a positively recognized and respected reputation as the number one executive and management level career consultant in the Southern California academic and business communities. To be achieved by providing the highest quality of career counseling, coaching, and job search strategies available anywhere."*

Poor Transition Planning

In today's global, highly competitive economic environment, the typical management or technical job lasts two and one-half to five years. That timeline is getting shorter. This means most of us must adapt to multiple jobs and career transitions throughout our careers.

"No job transition should begin without 40 hours of research," according to Richard Bolles, author of the best selling career series *What Color Is Your Parachute*. This research includes looking at your values, skills and interests as well as in-depth research on functions, industries and individual organizations. Once completed, the job hunter is able to describe their ideal job and develop and implement a plan to achieve it. Unfortunately only a fraction of individuals in job transition know how to plan a job transition or are too impatient to do the necessary personal and industry research.

Research ideally should focus on three areas:

1. **The targeted industry**, even if the job hunter has been in the industry over 20 years
2. **The major competition** in that industry, particularly the competitors of the job hunter's targeted companies. Often an individual's value to a company is in demonstrating how they can create a competitive industry advantage. A great way to do this is to approach the executives with a Special Report or a company specific proposal. I will get back to special reports and proposals later.
3. **The targeted companies.** This is the area where most job hunters focus and while important, alone it is not sufficient to get an offer in a very competitive economy.

"I believe that up to 95 percent of job hunters wing their interviews."

I routinely make this statement during presentations to senior executives and human resource managers. Then I ask, "By a show of hands, how many agree with what I just said?" Typically 80 percent of senior executives with hiring authority agree. I then ask, "By a show of hands have you ever winged an interview yourself and lost a position you really wanted?" Surprisingly over half of the executives and HR managers admit to winging interviews themselves.

How to Develop and Use Power Stories

As I write this, we are in the toughest job market since the great depression. Average will not get offers in this job market. Even good is not good enough to get management and professional offers. A candidate must be the outstanding individual among dozens to get an offer. The following technique for creating powerful stories for interviews will be helpful.

Suppose, as a marketing manager, your company had an underperforming consumer product. Your boss assigned you the job of developing a campaign to increase sales for the product. He gave you a six-month deadline and a limited budget. Despite these limitations, the marketing campaign you came up with resulted in a dramatic increase in sales. Here is how you would separate the elements using the **PAR** formula:

P (Problem/Situation)

Needed to create and implement an effective marketing plan for an underperforming consumer product and turn its sales around in less than six months on a $40,000 budget.

A (Action)

Worked 80-hour weeks for a month and a half to create and develop an innovative, cost effective marketing and public relations campaign using targeted radio spots and local newspaper ads.

R (Results)

The marketing campaign was implemented under budget in two months. Sales increased 35% in first six months and have continued to improve at this level for the last three years.

The next step is to rewrite your accomplishment in a concise manner. Use the following guidelines:

- Wherever possible **quantify your accomplishment**. This could represent increased revenues, money saved, time saved, man hours saved, etc. You can use exact figures or percentages or approximate the numbers if exact information is not available (i.e. more than 25%).
- Begin with **action words**, such as designed, developed, implemented, increased, saved, earned, etc.
- Keep each accomplishment **under 30 words**.
- When you rewrite the above accomplishment using these guidelines, this is the result:
  o **Created, developed and implemented** a consumer product marketing plan, on time and under budget that increased sales 35% in each of its first three years.
- If you worked with large sums of money, say millions of dollars, use the figure. If such were the case in the above accomplishment it might read:
  o **Created, developed and implemented** a consumer product marketing plan, on time and under budget that increased sales $35 million in each of its first three years.
- **Put the results up front**. To increase the impact of your accomplishment, put the **results (R)** at the beginning of the statement. For example:
  o **Increased sales $35 million** per year for three years by creating, developing and implementing a consumer product-marketing plan. The plan was implemented on time and under budget.
- **Try writing** twelve accomplishment statements. Whenever you doubt that an accomplishment is strong enough to be included, include it. Most men and women tend to undervalue their accomplishments. Once you have written the accomplishment you may find it stronger than you thought.

Completed Examples

- **Increased** occupational medicine patient volume 93% with projected net income of $325,000 by negotiating a worker compensation contract with McDonnell Douglas Government Aircraft Division.

- **Developed and implemented** a computer learning center which is projected to reduce outside vendor training cost 20% during the first year and 75% during subsequent years.
- **Conceived, designed and implemented** a three-year plan which secured degree granting status for a small British Columbia College. This required passing an act in the province's legislature.
- **Assisted** in raising over $400MM in equity within one week of issuance by preparing the prospectus and financial projection for the offering.
- **Earned recognition** for sales achievements by consistently placing first or second place in every promotion in the past 9 out of 10 years.
- **Generated** over $1 million annually by modifying and adapting a special instrumentation valve for an application for the semiconductor industry. The valve is now recognized as an industry standard.

Power Stories: three ways to approach the interview
- **Winging it:** The candidate is working out a story/example on the spot. This usually results in a lot of ahs, pauses and more often than not leaves out critical elements like benefits and bottom line results.
- **Sounding too rehearsed**: Interview responses at the second level can sound stilted, lacking a conversational tone and can come across as too rehearsed and phony. At this level, the candidate has rehearsed just enough to get out the facts but does not sound natural or conversational.
- **The confident expert:** In the third level the candidate has practiced their Power Stories so thoroughly that they come across naturally, conversationally and include critical elements and bottom line results. Obviously this third level takes the most practice but can pay huge benefits.

Create 3 X 5 Flash Cards
Once you have completed your Power Stories, put each story on a

separate 3 x 5 card. On the lined side write the story in about 30 words with the results as close to the beginning as possible. On the back of the card write one to three skills used in the story. You should prepare 10 to 12 flash cards, each with a different Power Story.

Use the cards as flash cards. Practice relating the skills to the Power Story until you can relate the story to the appropriate skill in a natural, conversational manner. Practicing for about an hour a day for about five days will make a dramatic difference in the number of callbacks and offers you receive following interviews.

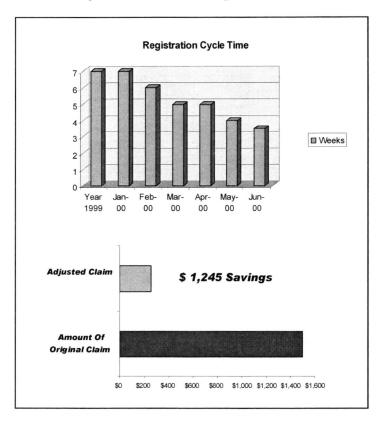

Relate It to the Organization

Several days after Derrick began his new job, he learned that the company had selected him because he demonstrated how his accomplishments would translate into increased market share for the company. To do this he used the phrase, "What this means to **(organization)** is ....," and then showed how each accomplishment translated to their bottom line.

To relate how your accomplishments transfer to an employer's bottom line the job hunter must do three things:

- **Research** using databases, directories, the Internet, and networking with fellow professionals at professional association and trade group meetings.
- **Write dialogue** that focuses on results and how those results translate into benefits for the target organization.
- **Rehearse** the dialogue to the point that it flows in an easy and natural manner.

If possible, create a simple graph. A graph can have an amazing impact when used in interviews, portfolios, special reports and proposals.

Former UCLA basketball coach John Wooden once said, "The harder I work, the luckier I get." In job search this is doubly true. If you take the time to prepare your Power Stories, research their benefit to your target companies, and practice telling them, you will dramatically increase the number of callbacks and offers you receive. This is because 95 percent of men and women don't work very hard at interview preparation and in effect wing job interviews. Increase your interview luck by using the technique outlined above.

222 Adapt or Perish

29

What happens when the recruiter calls?

By Mark Fierle

Now it's time to get into issues and tactics that can make you more attractive to an organization.

With an uncertain workplace recruiters and companies can be very selective with candidates that they choose.

The question for you is, "**What do you do when a Recruiter calls**?" First, take the call! Taking the call and the way you handle the ensuing conversation could greatly improve or hinder your career prospects. If the Recruiter has an assignment where your skills and background apply, you may even get an interview.

Here are four great ways you can ruin that opportunity:

1. **Being blasé** *about a meeting (face to face) with a recruiter. After all this is not a real interview. It's OK to go in* **dressed** *less than professionally,* **slouch** *during your meeting, and be sure after you make an off the wall remark to* **say***, "I would never say that during a real interview."*

A more **realistic approach** is to consider this as a real interview. Dress your professional best, come prepared, including a fresh copy of your resume and references, use good posture (sit up and look interested) and use good diction (speak concisely and in complete sentences). Generally, Recruiters are working on unadvertised positions that are "prime" in nature and great next steps for career-oriented candidates. How you come across to the Recruiter may have an influence on your career prospects. It can be through this assignment and future assignments the recruiter works on, or referral of you to one of their recruiter colleagues.

2. **Being** defensive **or unprepared when asked questions.** Most recruiters like to ask direct, pointed questions to ascertain your skills and accomplishments. A great way to make sure they do not find out about the real you is to evade the question...right? If they persist, tell them to refer to your resume; after all, it did take you two hours to put together!

A **far saner** approach is to be prepared to answer the question in a clear concise manner, **follow up** with a question like, "Have I made myself clear or would you like me to continue?" Never, ever refer to your resume other than as a reference tool for your own use. This approach requires a great deal of soul searching, starting with an inventory of your professional skills and a list of things you have done during your career of which you are most proud.

3. **Don't hesitate to fudge on your resume** (you know...exaggerate a bit). After all, it's common knowledge that everyone does it, and nobody ever checks up on it. Some good ways to do this are: show you have an advanced degree (even though you never finished your thesis), take full credit for something someone else did, or be liberal with employment dates. Keep in mind that these white lies can get you terminated.

4. **Don't be** realistic **about salary, job title, or responsibilities.** After all, don't we all want to get the most? It doesn't really matter that we are asking for the moon!

Don't risk blowing yourself out of the water by being obstinate or unrealistic. If your skills and background warrant title or compensation...you'll get it! Being unrealistic will legitimately cause the recruiter to question your judgment.

Experienced recruiters can be an invaluable resource, but they first must be sold on you. Your credibility and attitude helps them a lot with their clients. It's their decision who gets the interview. How you present yourself will determine their interest and your future opportunities.

Note: These criteria will also take you out of the running with a company that has contacted you directly. So be smart and do the right thing!

"I often ask candidates if they are getting calls from recruiters or people they have worked with in the past or have met at industry affairs or networking functions. If the answer is NO, I give them the following list of 10 things you can do to get back on their list!

"Have you had a call from a head hunter recently?"

So goes the ad from a local university promoting their Bachelor's and MBA program to working executives. The implication is that if you have one of these, head hunters and others will call with great opportunities!

I won't disagree that having a Bachelor's or MBA will open doors, but if you are feeling left out, here are 10 traits that will attract their attention:

1. Be a Strategic Thinker

In effect, this is simple. Just get to know all phases of your business. But be careful… you may also get calls, raises, and promotions from the "bigwigs" in your current company. Not bad, huh? Not easy though. It takes a lot of work.

2. Tolerance for Change

Get comfortable with change and uncertainty; it will always be with us so you might as well get used to it. I hear too often from candidates that they're "looking for a 'stable' company." Really?!

3. Show Ability to Lead Change

Look for these opportunities so you can say you did it. That is a powerful trait, and this attribute will cause your phone to ring, so check your voice mail! Or buy a Blackberry or iPhone and learn to tweet and make posts on Facebook.

4. Technology Awareness

Take the time to learn about new technology. This opens up possibilities when you become the "expert" on something that can take your company to the next level. Naturally others will hear about your deeds when this occurs. Note: Maybe you better upgrade your voice-mail options.

5. Intellectual Curiosity

Advance your education, attend seminars/conferences, get that MBA, go to school at night, get Certified/Accredited...etc! Show these certificates and list them on your resume. This is what's known as "being able to demonstrate." A famous entrepreneur said, "People rate you not by what you think you can do but by what you have done!" Be able to show them and good things will happen.

6. Self Reliance

Learn to trust yourself in your ability to deal with people and adversarial conditions. You will have plenty of opportunities to utilize this trait as you move up. It's never too late to learn!

7. Teamwork

Learn to work with diverse groups. Demonstrate the ability to assemble and tear apart groups. This is one of the most important "constants" head hunters will get from their clients. Your name will be on a lot of people's lips when you become known as a "team player."

8. Integrity

"Honest" and "Ethical" - these are things our mothers taught us (thanks Mom!). It is no less sought from clients that have "higher" standards - the type with which we all want to be associated.

9. Ability to Communicate Clearly

Be able to convey your ideas persuasively. Be comfortable with people from all backgrounds and levels. It is important that you hone both your verbal and written skills. Take writing classes. Learning to be an excellent writer will enable you to maybe even get something published. When you get published in a trade publication or newspaper this will define you as an expert and people will call you for advice. They even may ask you to speak on the subject-wow! Improve your public speaking skills by joining Toastmasters. Being a competent speaker along with taking writing classes will go a long way to improving the raw talent you have. Both are learned skills.

10. Service/Customer Oriented Mindset

Develop a perspective that you are a person who expects more and gives more.

If you want calls about opportunities, develop and refine these attributes and skills. A good way to start is to do an assessment of how you stand now. Rate each L (low), M (medium), or H (high). Then prioritize the top three that you rate yourself the least. Next, develop a game plan to improve these three. Then go on to the next three, and so on. Another essential is to get a mentor/boss to also rate you on each. This will give a perspective of how others think of you. Good luck, and have you upgraded your voice mail, how about your Facebook page and blog?

Next let's talk about the skills and attributes that are universal for interviewing. Here are:

6 Proven Steps to Getting and Keeping the Interviewer's Attention

It is not rare for a candidate to literally pat themselves on the back when they get an interview, then proceed to blow it during the interview. They worked hard to get the interview and think they can "wing it" and still do their job. Wrong! Getting the interview is the easy part, getting the job offer is the hard part.

Today, after years of corporate downsizing and job-shifting, the candidate pool has become inundated with semi-professional interview types. The competition is stiff and the message is: be prepared to outperform your competition. "Winging it" just won't get it done.

Use tried and true sales skills to attract interest and keep the interviewer's attention, even if you aren't a salesperson. Now that does not mean we have to develop new skills or become a salesperson, just refine some of our existing skills. After all we are always selling something whether it's to our supervisor, peers, spouse, children, or friends.

Here are six steps to get and keep the attention of the interviewer:

1. **Organize your thoughts before you start talking.** Muddled thinking serves a confusing message. If a thought is not clear in your mind, it is going to sound worse when you speak it. Interviewers don't want to struggle to understand you. Instead of blurting something out just take a moment.

2. **Get right to the point**. One of the most effective ways to lose an interviewer is to have them asking, "So what's the point?" Give the interviewer the "meat" in clear, concise language. They can chew on this while you elaborate with details. If they wanted to be kept in suspense they could watch a mystery movie!

3. **Translate your message into benefits for them.** People seldom ignore what you are saying if there is something in it for them. As the old saying goes, people like to stay tuned to their favorite radio station: WII-FM (**What's In It For Me**)!

4. **Ask questions to involve the interviewer.** Ask questions to find out what they are looking for, how you can help them, what is the biggest problem they are facing today, what are the most important priorities they would like you to attack. This will provide two things for you: It will tell you whether they are still listening, and secondly it will enable you to focus in areas that are of most importance to them. Interviews should be a two-way dialogue…not a monologue!

5. **Don't be afraid to let the real you shine through.** Companies don't hire resumes, they hire people. Each of us is unique with a unique personality; a blend of traits, thought patterns, and mannerisms. You weaken your communication when you try to say things in an unfamiliar manner. Instead of trying to copy a style that may not work for you, focus on what you are saying and to whom you are saying it. You will be more convincing and more comfortable.

6. **Be enthusiastic**! If you are not excited about your product (you), how can you expect the person you are interviewing with to be interested? Be animated, be lively! Add some enthusiasm to your dialogue and you will have more impact.

Make an effort to find what value you can bring to the company, be clear and concise, bring your uniqueness to the front, and show enthusiasm.

Let's now talk about the actual interview.

"The Eight Step Interview Process for Candidates"

1. Strategy

Typical Interview; Takes from 30 minutes to more than one hour and can influence your career for years to come. It's well worth it to prepare for the interview.

Objective: To convince the interviewer you are the best qualified candidate. To do so you will need to *sell* your qualifications, and skills.

Selling: We "sell" ourselves every day. It doesn't mean we have to develop new skills, just refine our existing ones. Find out what they need and show them how your qualifications, skills, and abilities are the best for the job.

The sales approach requires:
- Researching the company
- Reviewing your skills, experience, and accomplishments
- Revising your resume to emphasize the most pertinent items

2. Anticipate Answers

You should always anticipate your answers to questions they are most likely to ask. Some possibilities might be:

- *Tell me about yourself?* – Take no more than two minutes for your response. Include work experience, education, interests, and hobbies. Also, use this as a format to ask the interviewer about their needs.
- *What are your goals for the long term…short term…?* – The interviewer will be interested to see if your goals are ambitious or realistic.
- *What are your greatest weaknesses?* – Remember, negatives do not get jobs. Structure your answer to turn negatives into strengths.
- *Why do you want to leave/ why have you left?* – One possible reply would be, "I heard there was an opportunity…" If you were terminated, be careful not to talk negatively, explain factually. Turn it to the positive, "despite the problem, I learned a lot from the job"
- *What is your current salary/ what salary are you asking for?* Avoid answering questions about salary on the first interview unless you are actually offered the position and are considering accepting it. If you are asked specifically, try saying, "I'm really looking for the right career opportunity. I'm sure you will make me a fair offer if you want me." If you are pressed, you can respond with, "I believe on the basis of what I've accomplished, I would be entitled to some increase, but I would rather consider what you think I'm worth to the company."

3. Plan to Ask Questions

Ask questions during the interview as well as answering those asked of you. Be sure you answer questions directly, clearly, and concisely. Don't try to beat around the bush or try to avoid the question. Some to include are:

- Ask about the company and its products. Show your interest!
- Ask about how they plan to use your skills/background. Such as, "How can I help you the best? What do you want me to accomplish in the first 90 days? What is the biggest problem you would like me to tackle?"
- Ask about the people who previously held the position and where they are today. Illustrate your interest in the company's future. This can help you determine if this is a good decision.
- Ask questions about the importance of this position and your duties and responsibilities. Indicate that you are **goal oriented**.

4. Questions to Avoid

Until the job is offered, avoid asking questions about *benefits, vacation, retirement,* and *salary. They are not important until they want you.*

5. Appearance

Visual first impressions are very important. Consider your personal grooming and hair. Be conservative with after-shave, colognes, and perfumes.

As for dress, you are safer to be on the conservative side. Try to appear as businesslike as possible. For people on the interview circuit, I always recommend purchasing an "interview suit/outfit."

6. The Interview

Plan to arrive about 15 minutes early. Carry a briefcase or portfolio with several fresh copies of your resume and examples of your work.

Be sure you know the correct spelling and pronunciation of your interviewer's name. Greet your interviewer with a firm handshake and maintain direct eye contact at all times. Excellent posture, sitting or standing, is the order of the day.

7. Attitude and Tone

In any interview situation your attitude and tone of voice will have a great impact!

Strategy: Show how your qualifications, experience, and abilities relate directly to the company's needs.

Tactics: Always conduct yourself as if you are determined to get the job you are discussing. Never close the door on opportunity by being less than determined. Answer all questions positively and enthusiastically.

8. Close with Enthusiasm

When you sense the interview is about to end try to summarize a few *key credentials* and stress your interest in the job and the company.

Strategy: You do not want to play "hard to get." If you are interested you need to express your interest with enthusiasm.

Tactics: If you're interested, say so! If the job is offered, be prepared to accept it! If you are not ready to accept, ask for a day or so to think about it. If no offer is made, ask for a second interview. Be sure you get a business card. You will need it for the follow-up.

After the interview there are two things you need to do:
1. Review
2. Write

Review what happened within one hour after the interview. Put these thoughts down on paper while they are still fresh in your mind. Write down names of people you met and their job duties. Also include any identifying characteristics of the people you met with. This will help you recognize them in future meetings.

Jot down parts of the interview that you thought went well and those that caused you problems. This process will be very helpful in preparing for the second and any future interviews.

Finally (without delay), send a brief *thank you* note to the main participants in your interview. Be sure to include the following: the fact that you enjoyed the meeting and learning about the company, the fact that your background can definitely be of benefit to them, and that you look forward to discussing some ideas you have thought about since and tell them you look forward to discussing these at a meeting in the near future.

Here is some advice about nerves. It is normal for a person to be somewhat nervous before going on an important interview. We are all human and even the interviewer can have the jitters. Most of the time, it is a good thing. They help get our adrenalin going. They used to say that Joe Namath of the New York Jets would throw up before every game. The same was true for Jerry West, "Mr. Clutch" of the Lakers. There are many ways to handle interview nerves. My best advice is come in prepared. As a great golfer friend of mine says, "The more I practice (prepare) the luckier I get!" If you tend to get butterflies, preparation helps make those butterflies fly in formation! That's good advice for any stressful situation.

This next section is devoted to talking about job changes.

"Exit Statements vs Lame Excuses" What do I say about job changes?

How many seemingly lame excuses have we heard from executives who have recently been terminated from their jobs? With the increasing number of mid-senior level executives having two, three, even four jobs over the past ten years, the number of lame excuses has risen in direct proportion. When recruiters and hiring managers ask, it has almost become the thing to say, "I was part of a lay-off," or "I was re-engineered," merged, out-placed, excised, and right-sized or any number of sayings of the time.

As an Executive Recruiter I would rather hear a candidate say "I was fired." Why, you ask?

First, for the respondent using the "sayings of the times," there is an implication of "sympathy" – almost woe-is-me, life sucks, I'm a victim, or any other number of "feel sorry for me" implications. Another way to look at it is we're not happy in life all the time. We have to get out of the "woe-is-me" mode and find the opportunities ahead for us. Who wants to bring a sad sack into their company?

For an Executive Recruiter or hiring manager charged with finding "top talent," these sound like lame excuses and can mean even more "mediocre" talent. After all, even though it *does* happen, when does a company get rid of its best talent?

Second, it's almost refreshing to hear something different like, "I was fired!" When a candidate is honest enough to say these words, I'm almost anxious to hear the story behind them. After all, a person *can* be fired for the "right reasons."

Concerning "right reasons," some time ago a respected person in the career business told me "if a person is not fired at least once before they are fifty, they are not making enough waves!" The implication being that the person is either a trouble-maker or a risk taker looking for opportunities until he ran into a gunslinger with a bigger gun. We all realize that resistance to change is common in both people and companies, and the risk taker with new ideas to bring improvements is the most vulnerable. What then becomes important is the story behind the ouster.

Quite frequently, the average executive that gets laid off is the one taking the safe highway, accustomed to staying out of the way, just doing his or her job on a day to day basis. These are people who are rarely innovative and rarely expanding their networks either within or outside the company, industry or discipline. They work the hours, are perceived as dedicated and loyal and are long gone when there are downsizings, mergers, or whatever.

Of course, there are other reasons for getting fired that are less honorable. Here are some solid considerations for candidates that have left their jobs: it's often the best advice to be careful what you say and to whom you say it. It's better to say nothing during this period until the emotions have quieted down. This gives you time to calmly and unemotionally prepare an **exit statement** – a very important task, but one that is generally ignored or poorly prepared.

An exit statement is simply a *short and sweet* statement that you write and that your former employer or peers can verify. Keep in mind that when talking with a potential new employer or someone in your network, "why you left" will not be of any help in getting you a new position. The tendency is to spend too much time on the issue, and if you do, you will have less time to spend on the new issues that are of interest to your potential new employer. An example: it's much better to talk about the skills and experience you bring that can be of value to them.

Often it sounds like sour grapes when you go on and on about the rotten deal you got from your former employer. And believe me…people who have not prepared an exit statement, go on and on…and on…. So get that exit statement prepared and eliminate those lame excuses.

234 Adapt or Perish

Afterword

By VaNessa Vollmer, Psy.D.

This book was inspired by my efforts to apply the knowledge from my formal education to business and life. I share these obstacles and hard-earned insights and lessons with you in hopes of eliminating or softening the knocks and giving you hard-earned strategies that I and others have found to work.

One of my mentors was a big advocate of critical thinking. As a young person watching sitcoms on television, I was amazed and somewhat intimidated at the way the kids and young adults came up with witty comments, dealt with challenging situations, resolved these issues, and returned to a better life, all within 30 minutes. By comparison, it made an evolving young person feel inferior.

I talked about this concern with my mentor, who said, "Stop and think critically about this. Where were you when you were watching this program? Stop and think critically." I was inside the situation with the television characters and found myself wanting by comparison. "Okay, now step outside and describe the whole event in detail again." In doing so I now saw myself as a person watching a TV program. Going deeper, I now imagined the development, production and the acting out of the program. These actors were not real young people in a spontaneous situations, they were actors reading lines that they had been practicing, not lines which they had spontaneously expressed, but lines developed and refined by experienced writers in their 40s or 50s. Aha! This insight from closer analysis helped allay at least one blow to my teenage self esteem. Just like the mentor who helped me gain insight on my teenage angst, I thought it would be useful for those of us with hard-earned insights to pass them along to others venturing into today's complex world of business and life.

Sharing these insights may seem like a high aspiration. In discussing these topics with other business entrepreneurs and professionals from different arenas in life in early September 2009, we decided to collaborate on this book.

After reading this book and the insights we share, think about the experiences and insights you have had that you think would help mentor people. Please feel free to send them to us in care of the publisher so we may consider them for inclusion in a future version of this book.

As students of life, we have learned that all achievement begins with and eventually becomes reality from one thing, an idea.

The idea behind this book gelled as we discussed trends associated with earlier glitches in the economy: the odd/even gas days of the 70s, the mid 80s dip, the dot-com era of the 90s, and the early financial crises of this millennium. We saw how, through adaptations, mergers and acquisitions, the economy went from local to internationally outsourced almost overnight. We discussed books from the 1980s including Alvin Toffler's *The Third Wave*, and John Naisbitt's *Megatrends* coupled with psychology, leadership, success and business resources.

Having experienced the benefits and value of mentoring in our lives, we created this book because of our desire to understand the changes in this new economy and a desire to help others understand what they need to do to succeed, to help them deal with loss, hardship, and change, and to champion new opportunities for continued growth. Through this collaborative project, I and my co-authors leveraged each other's strengths. This synergy has developed into this collection of thoughts, tools and insights that will help individuals and organizations adapt to the global business paradigm shift. We offer this classic mentoring wisdom, tested through time, on a foundation of experience that will inspire generations to come.

It is great to have an idea. However, without a process to implement it, it usually remains just that...an idea. Good or bad, simple or complex, some ideas are better than others because they work. Those are the ones that succeed.

Why? It is one thing for one person to work hard to achieve a goal. However, it is far more powerful to gather together the strengths of a group of people with enriched perspectives from their life experiences and the collective wisdom gained from their triumphs over challenges they have faced. We share with you these insights from challenges in life and business that arose from persistence, patience and understanding the Aha! Moments we all experienced.

It has been an opportunity and a privilege to work with other experts to discuss and offer proven plans, techniques and systems to help others successfully adapt in our new economy. Successful evolution arises from a common thread woven into a mosaic of learning what has worked, continues to work, and will work in changing times in the future, giving us a mentoring resource to share with those who desire to learn more. You could use the alternative of trial/error, studying failure and success, and trying to reinvent the wheel, but who needs that when you can streamline the process with better insights into doing business?

Learning vicariously from others is a wonderful way to share useful ideas. Leaders who give back to the community by mentoring others create synergy. At an early age, I learned that it is rare to get much value or great insights from younger peers. Wise leaders, who have experienced failure and success and understand why both happened, are valuable resources those open to mentoring and vicarious learning can tap into. After all, no one needs to break a bone and go through the healing process to understand that it hurts when you can learn this from someone else's unfortunate experience.

We authors have worked with executives through all levels of organizations. People's perspectives have enriched our lives. We learned from others, understand how they think, know where they got stuck, and have helped them get unstuck. As mentors, we can guide people to work toward what they desire and are willing to act upon by sharing tools that will help them lead productive, enriched and successful lives.

We authors have seen people in several walks of life assess and leverage their strengths, successfully match their personal values with the professional values of corporate, government, and non-profit organizations. When wise leaders leverage their strengths and those of their employees, it results in leadership success for organizations of all kinds.

Many people complain about things that don't work or are superficially jealous of others. This rarely yields results that contribute to the betterment of others or mankind. Positive psychology, optimism and hard work teach us that if we redirect that negative emotional and thought energy into achieving our goals to serve others, it means the difference between success and failure.

Challenges will continue to emerge in the future. Technology continues to improve and that will continue to change the way we function. We authors believe that you may find yourself needing to solve some of these issues. You can either hide your resources or you can seek a mentor who has had prior success addressing these issues. It is your decision to continue working toward success. We hope that you will use this book as a powerful mentoring tool in your life.

Many people compare the current economic downturn to the Great Depression, when lessons learned left a strong impression. Success grows from learning lessons of self sufficiency, innovation and providing for the possibility that this could happen again. We learned from what our mentors shared with us and encourage you to grow in these challenging times by using these classic principles that have stood the test of time while creating innovation in products, services, and diverse business ecosystems.

People may notice many changes. New business models are driving innovation. Natural curiosity and interest in and asking for guidance are signs of intelligence. Willingness to learn from what works well is a skill. This is not something we are all born with but we can learn it and use it as we go through life, not just to survive but to evolve, gain confidence, and thrive.

Growing up in a community, we shared extra fruit from trees in our yard, and veggies and tomatoes from the garden like most others who had gardens and trees that produced more than enough for their own families. It made sense. Why let it go to waste? We made sure it didn't go to waste and shared the fruits of our labor with others to enjoy.

As the fruits of learning and labor were shared with our local community then, it makes sense to share these beneficial thoughts, insights, and lessons with others to enrich their lives now. This book was written to inspire all who want the opportunity to learn, adapt, and be mentored to build the creativity, innovations, and leadership values that have made the American Dream real in so many lives.

"Evolution is the cry of the mind. It is the scream of the intellect, urgency of the personality. Let us evolve!" ~Swami Abhedananda

"Change is constant, knowledge changes us and every thought affects our brain at a molecular level. Continue to learn and mentor others!"
~ VaNessa Vollmer, Psy.D.

Meet the Authors

Steve Amos
Business Consultant, Engineer

Steve Amos is a LCPT ME with Boeing and an entrepreneurial consulting wizard with Pax-CC. He has a diverse background as a product manager, project manager, mechanical manufacturing engineer, business owner, speaker, author, marketing, real estate appraiser and investor. Steve coaches teams that Turn Your Visions into Profits through developing new products, problem solving, turnarounds, improving lean processes, and creating marketing focused on customer needs.

Steve Amos helped turn around a division losing $9 million annually to be profitable enough to be sold. Steve also co-developed several niche products, one created first year sales of $6 million. Experience includes Boeing, Pentair Water, Goldrush Realty Advisors, Black and Decker, Sargent Lock, Colt Firearms, UNC Resources, United Technologies, Eastman Kodak and small entrepreneurial companies.

Steve is an ex-president of Career Builder's fellowship at Crystal Cathedral, and active in career groups.

Mark Fierle
Master Gardener and Executive Search Professional

After graduating from Gannon University in Erie, PA, he worked in management of finance areas for two Fortune 500 companies and two large International companies.

After a number of years and after being promoted and transferred to the West Coast, he joined a large International firm. He was one of two Americans on the management team.

239

Next came a large service company starting as Administrative Assistant, VP Admin and later on became President and eventually Chairman of the Board.

After the company was sold- the field of Executive Search got his interest. Soon, he started his own Search Firm and began writing free lance articles on career issues for a division of the Wall Street Journal and speaking to networking groups and graduate level classes as a guest speaker. He continues to consult with organizations involved with career issues.

Over the years one of his long time interests has been gardening. A few years ago he applied and was accepted into the University of California Master Gardener Program. This certified volunteer based organization helps the citizens of our county with gardening and horticultural issues. Along the way he found an area of great interest - vegetable gardening; specifically Square Foot Gardening. Today he is a Certified Square Foot Gardener, trainer. As well, he speaks on Master Gardening issues and does workshops across the West, and on a limited basis around the world. He can be reached at mfassoci@aol.com

John Hall
Career Transition Coach

John Hall has coached hundreds of executives and management employees through career transitions. At Chapman University, he developed and taught the only graduate outplacement course in the nation. He also taught *Advanced Job Search Strategies* in the Graduate Career Counseling Program at the University of California, San Diego.

John has had articles published in *The Wall Street Journal's National Business Employment Weekly*, *The Alumni Newsletter for the Wharton Business School* and *the Orange County Register*. For two and half years, he hosted a talk show, *Career Strategies* on Talk2K.com. *Newsweek* Magazine referred to him in 2011 as "the John Wooden of career coaches." John served three years on the National Board of the Professional Coaches and Mentors Association and is a Past President of their Orange County Chapter.

Ilene Albert-Nelson
Senior Marketing and Sales Executive

Ilene Albert-Nelson is a senior marketing & sales executive who has a passion for creating and selling things to people. She is known for her paradigm shifting thinking with a focus on turnarounds, starting new businesses and managing high growth businesses.

Ilene has worked for companies from start-ups to Fortune 100 companies such as Johnson & Johnson, Avery Dennison and Hallmark and has developed new products and turned around businesses for them all. She is an unusual marketing & sales person because, while she has very strong fundamental skills in marketing and sales, she also has very strong financial and analytical skills. She has created multi-million dollar business and turned businesses from losing 20% on sales to making 20% on sales.

Ilene is known for really grasping what is going on with a business and getting it pointed in the right direction with the right business plan quickly while delivering profitable growth. Ilene has sold products to everyone from big box stores such as Wal-Mart, Sam's Club & Michael's Stores to Mom & Pop stores as well as customers all over the world.

Ilene has an MBA from Wharton and a BS in Packaging Science from Rochester Institute of Technology.

Lee Pound
Writing Coach, Editor, Book Publisher, Speaker

Lee specializes in editing and publishing books for consultants, coaches and other professionals who want to become the recognized experts in their markets. He is also the co-producer of the Speak Your Way to Wealth seminars presented each August in Southern California.

He is the author of seven books, including *57 Steps to Better Writing*, and *Coaching for the New Century*. He has written two novels and three family histories. His publishing company, Solutions Press, specializes in business publications.

He started speaking professionally in 1974. In the late 1980's he studied creative writing with Sol Stein, one of the premier book editors of the 20th Century. This led directly to the writing of his novels and to his becoming a writing coach and book publisher.

Murray Schrantz
Independent Sales Engineer

Murray Schrantz is a sales engineer who brings his skills in sales and marketing to clients who have demanding requirements for engineered materials and process technologies in their manufacturing operations. He has successful experience in marketing and management positions with both multinational companies (Pfizer, BP) and small to mid-sized companies. Providing engineered products and processes for both mature and emerging markets is his specialty.

In addition to his work responsibilities, he also teaches business classes at local colleges and universities and has been a guest lecturer and consultant to industry. As a former Army officer (Ranger), Murray has transferred his expertise in military strategy and leadership to the commercial marketplace.

Murray is also a community leader who serves as a mentor and educational advocate for children in the foster care system, child advocate and former board director for Court Appointed Special

Advocates, a board advisor for the Mariposa Women and Family center, fundraiser for the community medical clinic, and a West Point board member and admissions representative.

Murray earned his MBA from Pepperdine and has an engineering degree from the United States Military Academy at West Point.

VaNessa Vollmer
Business Success Coach

Organizational Development and Human Resources Professional VaNessa Vollmer is known for setting up professionals and organizations to succeed! She has successfully implemented Global Leadership Programs in Aerospace, HiTech Manufacturing Organizations. VaNessa has partnered with leaders in Corporate, Government, and Non-Profit organizations. She has a proven track record of analyzing business problems through solution focused resolutions that save time and put money back into the bottom line.

Successful one-to-one leadership coaching & development for C-level executives and support staff is strength. With her background in Human Resources, Information Technology, Training, Organizational Development and Psychology she draws from experience and knowledge to facilitate successful business processes. Professional Development from a practical approach that is driven in research based methods and results provide a platform to take business transactions to transformational success.

VaNessa is currently President in Toastmasters International and participated in other leadership roles in the community including Optimist International. As a violinist she previously played with the Fullerton and Irvine Symphonies and is a member of Southern California Philharmonic.

She supports retiring military as they successfully transition to Corporate America through the Marine Executive Association West at Camp Pendleton www.MEAWest.org.

She graduated from U.C. Irvine and completed her Doctorate degree at United States International University.

Emily Woodman-Nance
Consultant and Certified Career Coach

Emily Woodman-Nance has over 20 years of corporate consulting and management experience working with Fortune 500 companies. She has provided her consulting services to public municipalities, non-profit organizations and Fortune 500 companies such as Nissan, United Airlines and IBM.

Emily Woodman-Nance coaches executive to entry-level clients to achieve more fulfillment in their careers. She is the author of the ebook "Survival Kit for the New Job Market". For one and half years, she hosted a talk radio show, Career Quest on KUCI 88.9 FM. Emily is a former President of the International Coach Federation Orange County Chapter (ICF-OC). She also serves on the Long Beach Weed & Seed Re-entry Sub-Committee.

Emily developed and teaches the curriculum for the coaching segment of the Human Resources Certification Program at California State University, Long Beach. She is also a Consultant with DBM, a global career transition firm. Emily was part of the Community Event Leadership Team for the Long Beach city-wide "Connected Corridor" effort. She is an alumnus of the Leadership Long Beach Institute. She was featured on Fox LA Jobshop segment regarding her career coaching expertise and professional perspective of the current job market.